RAISED BED
Gardening

A Complete Beginner's Guide

T0382936

Quarto.com

© 2023 Quarto Publishing Group USA Inc.
Text © 2016 Tara Nolan

First Published in 2023 by New Shoe Press, an imprint of The Quarto Group,
100 Cummings Center, Suite 265-D, Beverly, MA 01915, USA.
T (978) 282-9590 F (978) 283-2742

New Shoe Press titles are also available at discount for retail, wholesale, promotional, and bulk purchase. For details, contact the Special Sales Manager by email at specialsales@quarto.com or by mail at The Quarto Group, Attn: Special Sales Manager, 100 Cummings Center, Suite 265-D, Beverly, MA 01915, USA.

ISBN: 978-0-7603-8368-1
eISBN: 978-0-7603-8369-8

Library of Congress Cataloging-in-Publication Data available.

The content in this book was previously published in *Raised Bed Revolution* (Cool Springs Press, 2016) by Tara Nolan.

Library of Congress Cataloging-in-Publication Data

Cover images: All Donna Griffith except Bren Haas (front top right); Marc Green, Arlene Hazzan Green, The Backyard Urban Farm Company (front top left); Shutterstock (back right)
Lead Photographer: Donna Griffith
Builder: Scott McKinnon
Illustration: Len Churchill

Photo Credits
Crystal Liepa: 14 (left)
Greg Maxson: 134–135
Jessica Walliser: 4 (bottom left)
Paul Markert: 13
Rau + Barber: 62–63, 188–193, 130–133
Shutterstock: 18 (top right), 20, 23, 42, 57 (bottom), 60 (top left), 86 (all), 90, 126 (top)

RAISED BED
Gardening

A Complete Beginner's Guide

Grow Everything from Herbs to Tomatoes in Your Own Custom Raised Beds

TARA NOLAN

NEW SHOE PRESS

Contents

Introduction

What Is the Raised Bed Revolution?

*When you hear the word **revolution**, what comes to mind? You probably think of the more common definition, which is "rebellion" or "uprising," right? But **revolution** also means "innovation" and "modernization." For the purpose of this discussion—and for this whole book, for that matter—let's focus on those last two words.*

The emphasis on eating fresh, local food over the past few years has really changed the landscape of our towns and cities. Not only are farmers' markets more popular than ever before, more and more people are deciding to put their green thumbs to the test and grow their own food at home.

This is where innovation and modernization come into play.

Raised beds aren't a new invention, but they have certainly become more prevalent with this movement to grow fresh produce. And they've helped to modernize the way we garden. In bigger yards, raised beds seem to have replaced the typical expanse of a veggie plot. What's more, gardeners have gotten creative over the years and are experimenting with different options. This burst of innovation means a raised bed may not be a typical rectangle shape built from timber.

In fact, raised beds can be made in all shapes and styles—rectangles, squares, triangles, and circles; ankle- and waist-height; wooden and stone construction. They can even be welded out of steel, aging to a nice rust-colored patina over time, or made out of corrugated sheets of steel inset in a wood frame. Creative DIYers are rescuing materials from scrap heaps, antique markets, behind sheds, and underneath decks to upcycle into raised beds. Commonly found items, such as washbasins, stock tanks, and recycling bins, are getting a new lease on life as ready-made gardens.

My first raised beds, ready to be installed in their new home. *Tara Nolan*

The first two raised beds filled with soil and ready to plant with garlic. *Tara Nolan*

As the types of beds have changed, so have their locations. Raised beds are no longer just confined to the backyard. They're appearing on front and side lawns of residential streets, spaces that were once reserved solely for grass or ornamental plantings. Homeowners are reaping the benefits of that extra space and growing food to feed their families. Often the front yard becomes the prime candidate for a raised bed because that's the spot on the property with the best growing conditions—lots of hot sun! But savvy gardeners are taking advantage of whatever locations they can find.

Raised beds also are appearing in school and community gardens as well as in botanical and public gardens—often with accompanying seminars to teach people how to build and plant them. And if you peek behind a restaurant or look at a local eatery's rooftop, there's a good chance you'll catch a glimpse of a variety of raised beds where chefs have easy access to fresh herbs and a host of other menu-worthy edibles.

You may have started to see a newer type of raised bed here and there. Called "enabling gardens," they provide accessible growing spaces and inspiration to those who have various limitations. They help people with cognitive or physical disabilities enjoy the peace, motivation, and satisfaction that come from gardening.

Raised beds have also become instructional tools. Inner-city organizations are pairing them with educational programming to teach children who live in dense, urban areas where food comes from. Urban grocers and farmers' markets show enthusiastic new green thumbs how to garden for the first time, inspiring them to test their skills with edibles. Then, at the end of the season, they teach excited gardeners what they can do with their fresh bounty by offering a range of classes, from canning and preserving to incorporating fresh produce into healthy recipes.

Food banks also have benefitted from the increased use of raised beds for growing edibles. Individuals as well as organizations and community gardens often donate their extra bounty to feed the less fortunate.

The increased excitement for growing edibles has resulted in more interesting varieties of plants available at local nurseries, garden centers, and grocery stores. Edibles that once had to be grown from seed are being introduced to the masses in the form of plants. And an increasing selection of patio plants allows those with minuscule spaces to grow everything from tomatoes to mini melons.

Which leads to one very important detail about owning raised beds: they prove you don't necessarily need a conventional yard to grow a row of tomatoes. Because you're filling raised beds with your own mix of fresh, nutrient-rich soil, they can sit on gravel, pavement, poor soil, rooftops—pretty much anywhere!

Yards that were deemed to be hostile growing environments, with hard-packed clay or even sand, as well as patio stones, driveways, and decks, are no longer off-limits. You can place a raised bed right on them and fill it with quality soil.

Some of the most interesting raised beds you'll see are actually built from kits. *Donna Griffith*

Vertical gardening has become a popular concept that enables eager green thumbs to grow up where there is limited space. Different wall contraptions that provide space to grow fresh greens, edible blooms, and herbs are basically micro-sized versions of raised beds set up vertically rather than horizontally to take advantage of a sunny locale.

The aim of this book is not to reinvent the wheel but rather to inspire you with tons of ideas, practical tips, and easy-to-follow project plans that will help you create your own raised beds—no matter the size of your space. And if you don't happen to be particularly handy, there's an entire chapter devoted just to you. There are endless options for upcycling materials, from abandoned basins to whiskey barrels. Really, the only limit is your imagination.

This book will also introduce you to experts who share their tips on topics ranging from soil to irrigation, growing throughout the winter, and attracting pollinators to the garden. Be prepared to be inspired by hundreds of images that are meant to show you what a wonderful addition raised beds can be to your garden.

So, whether you have a big yard or a tiny balcony, join the raised bed revolution and create a bed—or two or three!—that allows you to reap the benefits of a fresh, homegrown harvest.

Raised beds can be added to any backyard in a configuration that suits the available space. Built-in trellis systems provide no-fuss support to vining plants. *Hilary Dahl for Seattle Urban Farm Co.*

You don't even need to live on solid ground to have a raised bed. A balcony, terrace, or rooftop will do, provided you have the necessary growing conditions. *Marc Green, Arlene Hazzan Green, The Backyard Urban Farm Company*

Chapter 1

Raised Bed Basics

Benefits of Raised Beds

There are a multitude of benefits that come from using raised beds, from getting a jump on the growing season to creating ideal growing conditions.

Enjoy an earlier—or later—growing season Depending on the climate where you live, the soil in a raised bed thaws, drains, and warms up sooner in the springtime than the soil in gardens that are in the ground. This means you can get a head start on planting edibles, more specifically cool-weather crops, like peas, lettuce, and beets. You may even be able to plant heat-loving vegetables a little earlier with the help of shelter, such as floating row covers (see page 13) or cloches (small plant covers). Many gardeners don't realize that they can plant and harvest more than one crop during the growing season. Raised beds give you a head start and extend the season beyond the traditional time frame.

A cloche is a valuable raised bed accessory that can protect tender young seedlings from sudden temperature fluctuations in the spring—frost, snow, hail, and so on. It can also protect newly sown seeds from opportunistic squirrels and birds. A cloche basically acts as a mini protective greenhouse. You can use anything from a traditional cloche to yard sale and antique market finds, like old punch bowls and glasses.

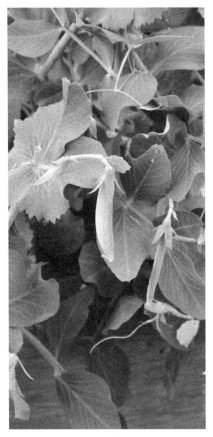

Peas are a great early season crop that you can be enjoying by the time you're ready to plant the heat-lovers, such as peppers and tomatoes.
Jennifer Connell

Control pests

Depending on the height of a raised bed, you can keep out smaller animals, including rabbits and groundhogs, because they won't be able to climb in. Various barriers can also be installed to prevent rambunctious pet dogs from messing up your garden and to keep out deer that might invite themselves into your yard for a snack.

A variety of materials, such as row cover and hardware cloth, can be added to a raised bed to keep out insects, vermin, and other pests. For example, row cover, added right when you plant your cabbages, can keep away

Protective cloches can be created out of any clear material, from plastic domes to cocktail glasses. *Niki Jabbour*

Special brackets have been added to the side of a raised bed frame to secure the hoops that will support a floating row cover. *Jessica Walliser*

cabbage moths and the cabbage worm eggs they lay. Hardware cloth, installed and secured at the bottom of a raised bed, will prevent moles, voles, and other digging rodents from attacking your crops from underground.

You don't want to pull up a fresh beet—or other root vegetable—only to find that a varmint has beaten you to that first bite.

Make crop rotation and companion planting easy

It's been proven that planting the same thing in the same place year after year is not good for the soil. Raised beds not only make it easy to keep track of what you've planted where each year, they make it easy to move crops around, which helps the fertility of the soil. Rotating crops also aids in preventing pests and diseases.

Companion planting is the method of planting edibles that will thrive and benefit from each other. Many new gardeners don't realize that some edibles simply do not play well together. This could

affect your harvest. Cucumbers, for example, do not do well when they're planted in proximity to potatoes, but they will tolerate being planted near nasturtiums, peas, and beans. On the other hand, some plants benefit greatly from being planted together. Basil, for example, is said to improve the flavor of tomatoes.

Planting beans, squash, and corn together is a perfect symbiotic match because sturdy corn stalks act as the perfect trellis up which the nitrogen-rich beans can climb, while the squash spreads outward, choking out any potential weeds.

You can plant groupings of edibles that belong to the same family, such as nightshade veggies— tomatoes, eggplants, and peppers—but sometimes there's an odd man out, like potatoes, which don't thrive around their tomato cousins.

A garden journal can help you keep all of this straight and keep track of what is placed where each season.

What Is Row Cover?

Ever had a problem with insect pests like cabbage worms? Are birds eating all the ripe berries on your trees or shrubs? Floating row cover is your new best friend.

Depending on the thickness, row cover will also protect your crops from weather fluctuations, ranging from frost to high heat. It can also shield them from the sun's harsh rays.

HOW TO USE IT: Row cover generally comes in a roll that can easily be trimmed to size with scissors. To protect delicate seedlings, you can add hoops (see Accessorize Your Raised Bed, page 43) to suspend it above the soil. Simply secure it with clamps to the edges of your bed, or use something heavy to hold it down—even tucking all the edges into the soil will do the trick.

Row cover, also referred to as floating row cover, is a lightweight material that can be used to protect crops from a variety of menaces. It allows air and water to permeate so that you don't smother what you're trying to shelter underneath it, and a great deal of light shines through it as well.

Row cover can help protect your newly sown seeds or freshly planted seedlings from marauding squirrels or a strong wind. It can also help speed up the germination rate of seeds.

LET THE POLLINATORS IN: While row cover can keep out the bad guys, such as cabbage moths, certain plants such as beans and peas need the good guys—pollinators!—to help those flowers develop into fruit. Once a plant starts to flower, be sure to lift away the row cover so bees and other pollinators can get to work.

Provide accessibility

Raising up the beds makes it easier for those who may have trouble bending over or kneeling down to plant and weed. Some raised bed designs, like the Raised Bed with Benches (see page 50), even provide a place to sit. Other designs can be customized to accommodate a wheelchair or scooter.

Increase yield

Not only will attracting pollinators to your garden boost your harvest, the very act of gardening in a raised bed can be of benefit to your seasonal bounty too. According to an Ohio State University Extension Fact Sheet, a raised bed that was studied over three years at Dawes Arboretum in Newark, Ohio, produced 1.24 pounds of edibles per square foot. That's more than double the yield of what is grown in a conventional garden!

Overcome bad soil

The soil conditions of some yards, such as hard-packed clay or excessive sand, might be discouraging to those who want to garden. You can amend these conditions over time, but putting a raised bed over bad soil allows you to bring in your own fresh soil and compost. Essentially you're controlling the environment of your raised bed. In fact, you don't need to place a raised bed on soil. Raised beds can sit on top of gravel, asphalt, or pavers because it's the soil you add to the beds that is going to be full of the nutrients needed to grow your plants. For example, if your driveway is a prime location because it's the only place that gets six to eight hours of sunshine a day, consider placing your raised bed along the side or across the top—anywhere that will still provide room for your car.

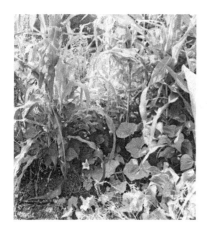

"The Three Sisters" is a popular label for the classic planting combination of corn, squash, and beans.

The Annapolis Royal Historic Gardens feature an Innovative Garden with several accessible raised beds that were designed to be senior- and wheelchair-friendly. *Trish Fry*

Garden in limited spaces

Living in an urban area does not mean having to forsake gardening altogether. There are many compact, creative raised bed alternatives that allow for growing edibles in small, challenging spaces, whether you have a tiny patio, a postage stamp-size lawn, or even a rooftop space or balcony.

Keep your garden tidy

Aesthetically, if you have a big space for your crops, raised beds allow you to keep everything neat and orderly. You can connect different beds with pathways lined with mulch or pea gravel, and you don't have to stomp into a growing area to reach the weeds. A great size for raised beds is 3 or 4 feet by 6 feet. This allows you to tend your beds without damaging the soil.

Allow for easy drainage

In yards with poor drainage, water may stick around and saturate a traditional garden after a heavy rainfall, harming the roots and promoting mold and disease. By raising up the bed and filling it with healthy, non-compacted soil, you provide a better opportunity for the bed to drain after a heavy rain. You can also add gravel or drainage holes to your beds to provide additional draining capabilities, depending on where your bed is placed.

Contain spreaders

Anyone who has ever innocently planted chamomile or mint in the garden and let it go to seed knows what a pain such a plant can be to control. You'll be pulling it out forever! Raised beds can provide a controlled environment that enables you to grow some of the spreaders you know and love but prevent them from taking over the entire garden. (That is, a small raised bed, where you don't plan on planting anything else ever again.) Why Garden in Fabric Pots (see page 123) offers some raised bed recommendations. We've also highlighted an octagonal raised bed that will contain strawberry plants, which are also enthusiastic spreaders (see page 110).

Reduce weeds

You can't help what weed seeds are blown in by the wind, what's dug into the soil by a squirrel, or what's dropped by a bird flying by. Even a soil delivery from a truck can inadvertently introduce a few weed seeds. However, by laying down landscape fabric at the base of your beds, you can smother any nasty

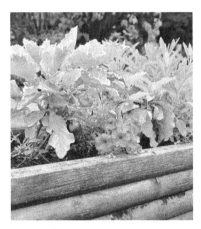

Mix in a few ornamental blooms with your edibles to lure beneficial insects into your plot. *Bren Haas*

It's not what's underneath the raised bed that counts; it's the soil you put inside. Therefore, this fabric raised bed is perfectly happy resting on patio stones. *Niki Jabbour*

Raised beds made from special fabric can be placed on the corner of a deck or balcony, on a small patio, or on a rooftop garden. This one, manufactured by Woolly Pocket, is made from 100 percent recycled materials. *Joshua White*

weeds that are currently in the ground and prevent them from creeping upward through the soil to invade your bed.

Grow a cutting garden

From spring through fall, something is always in bloom. What better way is there to celebrate the growing season than with a vase of freshly cut flowers? When you're planting your long-stemmed beauties—cosmos, dahlias, zinnias, coreopsis, gladiolas, and more—in your ornamental gardens, keep a few aside to go into your vegetable raised beds. They'll attract valuable pollinators and beneficial insects to your garden, and you can sacrifice the blooms for container arrangements.

Make a trial plot

If you're like many a green thumb who comes home from the nursery with more plants than originally intended, raised beds work well as holding areas until you figure out where to plant these extra, unexpected purchases. A corner of a bed can also be reserved for testing out a plant to see how it might perform (before putting it in the garden), to nurse a plant back to health if it hasn't thrived in another area of your yard, or to raise a mystery seedling until you know what it is (and ensure it's not an invasive weed).

Preserve your garden soil

Tromping through a traditional plot can harm the plants as well as compact the soil. Underneath the soil on the top of a garden is a web of organic activity. Raised beds protect all those vital underground processes, providing you a way to tend the plants without walking on the soil.

In addition, the sides of a raised bed ensure that everything stays in place. In a traditional garden, precipitation has the power to simply wash away your good intentions—and all your healthy soil. And while it's possible that heavy rain can deplete soil in a raised bed (as can a freshly pulled-out crop), it's easy to replenish.

Choosing a Size

As you will see throughout this book, raised beds come in all shapes and sizes. They're completely customizable depending on the gardener's specific requirements. However, these measurements are considered standard for a typical raised bed.

Length and width

The standard length and width of a typical backyard raised bed is about 3 to 4 feet wide by 6 to 8 feet long. This allows for easy access from all sides when you're planting and weeding. It's best to be able to reach into the beds from the side when you're working in them.

Technically, if you want to build one long raised bed, that's narrow in width (because that's what your space allows), you could do that, too, but you must be mindful of the fact that the sides can shift if you don't add supports every few feet.

Staking the side of a raised bed: the ground around your raised bed will shift and heave over time—especially after a rough winter. While it may be tempting to simply create a standard raised bed rectangle with stakes attached to the inside corners, over time you may find the middle of the longest lengths warping out or in, or shifting. One way to avoid this problem is to secure stakes to the outside of the raised bed, about halfway from the end, at the time of building. This should keep the boards firmly in place.

Height

The height of a raised bed can vary greatly. It might be waist-high or a little bit lower to accommodate a wheelchair, for example. Our raised bed on page 50 has benches installed, perfect for perching as you weed and plant.

Generally, though, raised beds are a bit lower to the ground. A standard rule of thumb is to make them about 10 to 12 inches high. However, if your

Adding a little reinforcement to the long sides of a raised bed will prevent them from bowing in or out over time. *Donna Griffith*

Benches attached to a raised bed provide a comfortable place to rest, but also to garden from. *Donna Griffith*

beds are really low and you're planting carrots, parsnips, or other root vegetables, for example, the plants are going to reach down into the subsoil that's beneath the raised bed. If the root vegetables hit the uncompromising soil underneath, they can become stunted and misshapen. Even plants that grow upward will have roots that travel downward, and they may hit the subsoil underneath. If that soil isn't healthy, or it's hard and compacted, it's going to affect the plants. There are measures you can take to amend the subsoil, such as double-digging and adding compost. But if you don't want to have to deal with the subsoil, simply increase the height of the bed a few more inches so your crops will be contained in the raised bed.

If you're upcycling an old container into a raised bed, make sure that the depth will allow for the roots of your chosen plants to flourish. A lettuce table, for example, is very shallow, so it's only suited to plants with equally shallow root systems. Deeper raised beds allow for all other edibles to be planted and to thrive.

Spacing between beds

The distance between your raised beds is also important. There should be enough space so that you can comfortably bend or kneel down to access the raised beds from the sides. If your raised bed is in a community garden or accessible by the public, you may want to make the spacing even wider to accommodate wheelchairs or walkers. If you'll need to maneuver a wheelbarrow between beds, you'll need to take that into consideration as well.

Choosing Raised Bed Materials

Just as the soil you choose is an integral element to creating a raised bed, so are the materials with which you choose to make them.

New wood For wooden raised beds, look for untreated, rot-resistant wood. The availability of certain woods at the lumberyard or home improvement center will depend on your location and what grows in your region. However, it's likely that the most common rot-resistant wood you'll find is cedar. Even most of the raised bed kits that you can order online come with cedar boards. Before loading up your cart with wood, be sure to check the price per board so you know how much your raised bed is going to cost. You don't want to be surprised with a budget-busting tab when you get to the checkout.

Look for the Forest Stewardship Council (FSC) stamp when you're purchasing your wood. It's an international certification and labeling system with standards that tracks where your wood has come from and promotes responsible forest management. When you purchase wood with an FSC label, you know it has come from a reputable source and has been properly harvested.

When you're building a bed with rot-resistant wood, the hope is that it will last several years before you have to replace rotting lumber. Some boards will unfortunately age faster than others.

Lining a bed with plastic can help prevent wood from rotting. The lining keeps the wet soil from touching the wood on the inside. Just be sure to only line the sides of the raised bed and not the bottom because the water needs to drain downward and out the bottom of the bed. To avoid rusting, you'll also want to use stainless-steel staples to fasten the plastic or landscape fabric to the bed.

Recycled wood Be careful when you're reusing wood that's come from another project. For example, you want to avoid using railroad ties and pressure-treated wood—especially if you're growing edibles—because the harmful chemicals they were treated with can leach into the soil: Until about 2003 or 2004, chromated copper arsenate (CCA) was used in the making of pressure-treated wood.

Because of past practices, current opinions vary on using the new pressure-treated woods that are on the market. At the time of printing, there is at least

Rot-Resistant Woods

- Black locust
- Black walnut
- Catalpa
- Cedar
- Chestnut
- Cypress
- Hemlock
- Ipé
- Osage orange
- Pressure-treated pine (non-CCA)
- Redwood
- White oak

Ask an employee at your local lumberyard if you have questions about what the labels on various types of lumber mean, as well as for raised bed wood recommendations.

When shopping for wood, look at the end of the board for more details about its origins and treatment. This label, for example, provides information about the type of preservative that was used, and the name and location of the treating company. A quick online search will reveal the answers to any questions you may have about the origins and treatment of certain types of wood.

one new brand of pressure-treated wood being sold that has environmental certifications. You may want to investigate these materials for yourself and decide what you're comfortable using for your raised beds.

If you're reusing old wood that has an old coat of paint on it, you need to be careful because the paint could contain lead.

Protecting wood Even if your raised beds are built from rot-resistant wood, they'll still deteriorate over time, and you may need to replace boards here and there. If you want to help prolong the life of your raised beds, you can treat the wood using an eco-friendly stain, although you may still want to confine its use to the outside boards if you're growing food in the bed. Some wood oils use natural ingredients and offer UV protection. Flaxseed

Wood preservative can be applied to just about any wood , reclaimed or otherwise, to help it better resist degradation from moisture or insect damage.

Choosing multiple paint colors adds a playful element to a raised bed space. *Amy Andrychowicz*

oil and wax are natural stains that can be used to protect the wood. Be wary of linseed oil, however; it can contain chemical additives that you don't want around your plants. Do a little research to find a sealer that you feel comfortable using for your raised beds.

Nonwood materials Some materials will simply last longer than wood. Old paving stones or bricks can be piled to create raised bed walls. Just be mindful of using a technique that ensures they're not going to cave in. As you would with old wood, if you're reusing concrete blocks, for example, be sure you know where they come from. Concrete blocks used to be called "cinder blocks" and were made with fly ash, which is a dangerous substance.

Make sure that whatever material you choose for your raised bed isn't going to leach dangerous chemicals into your soil over time. For example, one safe option is to have a professional weld steel into sturdy raised beds that will truly stand the test of time.

Soil for Raised Beds

Now that you've built your raised beds, you need to create a nourishing environment where your plants will grow and thrive.

Healthy, nutrient-rich soil is the number one ingredient to a successful raised bed. Within healthy soil is a web of organic activity created by a variety of microorganisms, such as bacteria, fungi, nematodes, and larger organisms including earthworms. They break down organic matter, leaving behind a trail of nutrients as they move through the soil. Plants absorb these nutrients as they grow and produce blooms and fruit.

You want to encourage and then feed and maintain this little ecosystem, and raised beds are especially helpful in this. One of their benefits is that they allow you to reach into the garden to weed and plant, rather than standing in it and harming these subterranean processes. Many gardeners even subscribe to a no-till method of gardening, meaning they don't disturb the soil at all, ever, once it's been established. They simply add beneficial materials to it and allow nature to work its magic by gradually incorporating the additions into what's already there.

This method is also said to promote better aeration and drainage throughout the soil.

Even the United Nations recently acknowledged the importance of healthy soil as it pertains to agriculture and food security by declaring 2015 to be the International Year of Soils. Here's a sample of what was written in the resolution:

> *Noting that soils constitute the foundation for agricultural development, essential ecosystem functions and food security and hence are key to sustaining life on Earth,*
>
> *Recognizing that the sustainability of soils is key to addressing the pressures of a growing population and that recognition, advocacy and support for promoting sustainable management of soils can contribute to healthy soils and thus to a food-secure world and to stable and sustainably used ecosystems.*

The right soil mix If you're building one or more larger raised beds for your yard, chances are it's more economical to arrange for soil to be delivered

Be sure to nurture your soil just as you do your plants. Healthy soil = healthy plants.

to fill them than buying soil by the bagful. Be careful what kind of soil you order. Topsoil typically won't contain all the wonderful nutrients that you'll find in a special mix, but if that's what you must use, you'll want to heavily amend it with compost or manure. Just be sure to find out where it has come from. A soil delivery company will also likely have different grades of soil, so choose the best one that you can afford. Look for the words "triple mix," which should have a healthy, well-screened mix of topsoil, peat, and compost.

Speaking of triple mix, if you're going to blend your own soil, a good rule of thumb is to mix ⅓ compost with ⅓ peat moss and ⅓ perlite or vermiculite. Mel Bartholomew, who invented the Square Foot Gardening method, recommends that five different types of compost go into that third.

You can also find special blends of container soils mixed specifically for growing edibles. These bags of soil are well-suited to filling a smaller raised bed that's on a balcony, rooftop, or other small space. Keep in mind that there won't be as much organic activity going on in soil that's on a balcony or roof, so it's important to fill your raised bed with the best-quality soil you can afford. You'll want to amend your soil frequently by adding a bit of compost or organic fertilizer to restore any nutrients that are leached out by constant watering.

Amending soil is also important when caring for a raised bed that's on solid ground. A topdressing of compost—about an inch or two—in the spring and fall is usually recommended, but a periodic topdressing throughout the season will work its way into the soil and help to feed it too.

Here are the three key ingredients to a healthy soil:

Compost: Compost is organic matter that has decomposed. Often called "black gold," it adds nutrients to the soil. Compost can come in many forms, from cow manure to a mixture of grass clippings, coffee grounds, and other kitchen waste. You can make your own using a compost bin, buy it in bags, or have it delivered. Compost can be used to amend poor soil, or it can be added to your raised bed soil mix.

Peat moss: Peat moss works on the texture of the soil, allowing it to retain nutrients and water that's slowly delivered to the plants.

Perlite or vermiculite: Both perlite and vermiculite help promote aeration and also work to retain moisture.

What is loam and humus?

Many gardening books and articles refer to having a "loamy" soil. Loam is that perfect balance of sand, silt, and clay in your soil, all ideal components to growing your plants. This is what the plants draw their minerals from. Too much of any of these ingredients, however, like too much clay, can create challenges when you're trying to grow certain plants.

Humus is all that beneficial, organic stuff that's left behind when things like leaves, sticks, and grass clippings break down. It contains a variety of nutrients, including nitrogen, which plants rely on for photosynthesis and growth. When added to your soil—or loam—it provides these nutrients, but it also helps to promote that web of activity mentioned earlier by making the soil more friable. A nice crumbly soil will help promote aeration and water retention as well as provide a nice environment for all those beneficial organisms that you want to attract so they can get to work in your garden.

Compost is the term used to refer to a manmade decomposition pile. We add our kitchen waste and yard detritus to make our own compost, while humus happens in nature. Essentially, humus is Mother Nature's compost. Both are beneficial to the garden.

How much soil?

Soil deliveries can be pricey, so you want to make sure that you calculate almost exactly how much soil or compost you'll need (with a little more added as insurance) so you don't need to place another order (and incur another delivery charge). To determine how much soil you need, measure the length, width, and depth of your raised bed and multiply those numbers together to get the amount of cubic feet of soil needed.

There are 27 cubic feet of soil (3 feet × 3 feet × 3 feet) in one cubic yard. To calculate how many cubic yards of soil you'll need, divide the amount of cubic feet by 27.

When you add the soil to your raised bed, fill it until it's almost 2 inches from the top. You'll find that the soil will settle over time. A strong rainstorm may flatten things out as well. You'll also want to replenish the soil whenever you pull out a fresh crop because harvesting can deplete the soil levels. To minimize this, try to shake the soil from the roots of any plants you pull.

If you do happen to order a little too much soil, spread it around your other garden beds, or save it to replenish your raised beds later on in the season.

Location and Site Maintenance

Choose the right location

You've decided you want a raised bed. Now, where should you put it? Basically, it needs to go where the most sun is, especially if you're planting edibles. You want your bed to receive at least six to eight hours of sunshine per day.

Before choosing the "forever home" for your raised bed, assess the space you're considering over a couple of days—perhaps over a weekend—and record when the sun hits the space as it moves from east to west. Keep in mind that if you record your sunniest spots

in the spring before the leaves have appeared, your chosen area may get a bit more shade throughout the day as the season progresses.

You don't necessarily need an area with grass or soil for raised beds. They can also be placed over hard surfaces such as concrete or pavers.

Try to be a bit strategic when you're planning which direction your raised bed will face. You want to make sure that all the plants in it will enjoy the sunshine. So when you're digging in your seedlings, don't plant the tallest veggies like pole beans or even tomatoes where they're going to cast shade over shorter plants. If there are little spots of shade here and there, you can underplant with veggies that can tolerate shady spots, such as spinach and lettuce.

If your garden is facing the street or you just want it to look tidy from the yard, plant a few ornamentals along the border. Marigolds are good pest preventers, as are nasturtiums (they're edible too!), which will cascade over the sides of your beds as they grow. Other plants like zinnias not only are pretty, they also attract pollinators.

You might also embellish the bed with paint or layers of wood, as we've done with the upcycled bed design on page 46.

Adding a raised bed to a slope

If your optimal sunny spot happens to be on a slope or uneven stretch of ground, leveling out your raised bed will keep your yard looking neat, and the bed will look as if it's always been there. An easy way to level out your bed—especially if you've built it with stakes in the corners—is to dig in the length that's closest to the slope. Start by putting the lowest corner in the ground and then, using your level, keep measuring the sides as you lift and dig in accordingly. Use soil to shore up the sides or cut pieces to fit bigger spaces that are exposed, and use a stake placed on the inside of the bed to attach it to the whole structure.

Three Reasons Why You Should Own a Compost Bin if You Have Raised Beds

1. Cut down on household waste. You can divert up to 30 percent of your trash by sending it to the compost bin instead of the garbage can.

2. Create nutrient-rich soil. Your garden will benefit immensely from the "black gold" that you create in your compost bin.

3. Save money. Organic compost can be pricey, so free is even better!

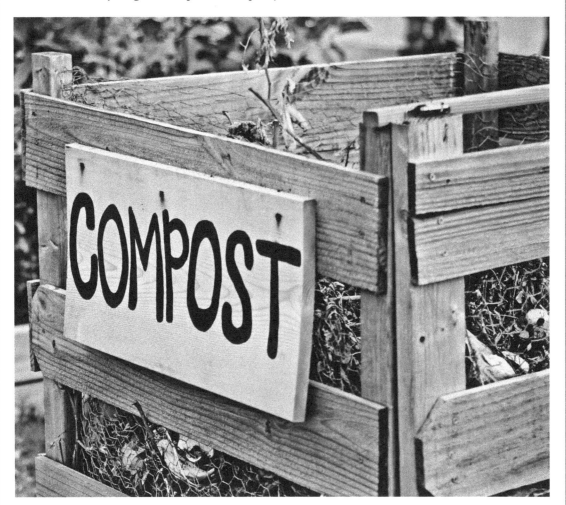

A compost bin is a valuable asset to any garden because it will produce ample amounts of "black gold" all season long—provided that it's regularly filled with organic matter and yard waste. This also benefits your garden budget because you won't have to worry about purchasing the compost from elsewhere.

Prepping the site

Lay gravel for drainage If you're placing your raised bed in an area that doesn't drain well, you may want to place a layer of gravel in the bottom of your bed and even around it so the water can more easily move away from the bed. This will help prevent the bed from rotting and mold from forming. It will also help the soil itself to dry out.

Remove grass from a site Removing sod isn't an easy task, but you only have to do it once. Mark the area where you want to place your raised bed. Include room for pathways, if you want a delineated space between the grass and your raised bed. Use stakes and string to outline the perimeter where you need to dig. Use an edger or a sharp square spade to cut the sod into easily removable chunks. Some municipalities do not allow discarded sod to be placed in compost bags, so you'll need to figure out where to dispose of it.

The cardboard trick Digging up grass probably isn't at the top of your landscaping list of tasks because it can be difficult and time-consuming to pick up chunks of sod piece by piece. However, if you plan ahead you can avoid this onerous task by placing cardboard over the area for the raised bed. Then cover the cardboard with a layer of soil. The cardboard will kill the grass and break it down, leaving fresh soil in its place. If you do this in the fall, your new garden should be ready by spring. Otherwise, lift up a corner after a few weeks to see if the grass has started to break down. This process also makes it easy to add a pathway. Simply add a layer of landscape fabric to your newly decomposed area and top with the path material of choice, such as pea gravel, straw, or mulch.

It may be time-consuming, but you can systematically turn over the sod to make way for raised beds.

Tips for Dealing with Slopes

The following tips for dealing with a slope are from Ian Wilson of Portland Edible Gardens. If you have a sloped area that happens to be exactly where you want to place your raised bed, there are a few things you can do to accommodate a new garden. Photos by Ian Wilson

RIGHT: In cases that require or recommend building down the contour, it's often helpful to terrace or step raised beds incrementally to account for the slope. This method, though more involved, makes for an elegant and aesthetic design.

BELOW: Building raised garden beds on slopes is always challenging. The easiest approach is always to orient raised beds along the contour of the slope. This requires the least amount of excavation and grading of the terrain prior to installation.

Raised bed maintenance

Over time, harsh winters and general wear and tear can cause your beds to heave, resulting in uneven boards. Even rot-resistant wood will break down over time. Check your raised beds in the springtime for rot, and replace any deteriorated boards that are easy to disassemble from the frame with new boards.

You also should check for any boards that bow out. You may have seen raised beds with stakes along the longest sides. They can be unsightly, but they really help hold the boards in place. To add a stake, drive it into the ground about halfway along the outside of the frame. (See Essential Raised Bed, page 38, for an example.)

Feed the soil Continuous watering of your raised beds throughout the season naturally leaches the nutrients out of the soil. In addition, the plants are also absorbing nutrients from the soil and using them to grow. As a result, you need to regularly give your soil a little boost, either by adding an organic fertilizer such as kelp or by spreading fresh compost on the top of the soil.

Rotate crops One of the benefits of having multiple raised beds is that you can easily move your crops around from bed to bed each year. This is called "crop rotation." Farmers use this method to manage the fertility of the soil in their fields. Continuously planting the same crop heavily depletes the soil. Even in a home garden, crop rotation is important for a variety of reasons—it helps to minimize soilborne diseases and pests, and it helps you manage the nutrient levels and fertility of the soil. Try to move different families of vegetables around.

Prepare beds for winter

As you complete your autumn gardening tasks throughout your entire yard, there are a few things you can do to tuck in your raised beds for winter.

- Once you've pulled out and composted all the spent plants, add a few inches of compost to replenish the beds.

- Keep your leaves! Leaf mold is a great soil amendment ingredient. If you have the space, keep a pile where they can break down over time. Or if you want to use some leaves right away, run over them a few times with a lawnmower to break them up, and then add a layer of them to your raised bed. The earthworms will love you.

- Don't, however, add a big pile of large leaves to the garden. They can become moldy and smother the soil rather than enhance it. If you notice any diseased leaves, be careful not to add those to your soil. And don't use leaves from a black walnut tree. They contain juglone, a toxic chemical that many plants do not like.

- If you've planted garlic or cool-weather root crops that you'll be harvesting throughout the winter, lay down a layer of straw (not hay, because of the seeds) to keep things nice and cozy.

- Remove any plant supports, trellises, or garden ornaments, clean the soil off of them with an old cloth, and store them.

- If you have removable row cover hoops, you may want to install them in the raised bed and keep the row cover close at hand. That way, if there's a sudden frost warning, you can run outside and cover up any crops that need protection.

- Keep a small shovel or brush handy to brush snow off cold frames or row cover.
- For balcony beds, remove and discard the soil completely so that you can start fresh in the spring. The freeze and thaw cycles of the winter can wreak havoc on smaller beds, causing the wood to heave or crack.

Plant cover crops

A cover crop is a crop that's planted to help replenish and improve the soil between plantings. For example, once garlic or any cool-weather crop is harvested (often in mid-summer), there's an empty space left in the garden. Cover crops can be planted there. They're fast-growing and return nutrients to the soil once you dig them under. That's why they're also referred to as "green manure" because essentially you're growing your compost.

Buckwheat is a popular mid-season cover crop. It matures within 70 to 90 days, helps to keep the weeds down, and attracts beneficial insects to the garden. Just be sure to turn it under before the seeds form.

Fall is a great time to grow cover crops because you've reaped most, if not all, of your harvest and the beds are just laying bare, waiting for spring. Peas and clover work well because they add lots of nitrogen back into the soil. Winter wheat and winter rye are also popular choices that can be planted in fall and dug into the soil a few weeks before you want to plant your first spring crop.

Keep construction to a minimum

If you don't consider yourself particularly handy, specially made corners allow for a quick and easy raised bed setup. Simply lay out your wood cut to the lengths that you want as well as the decorative corners that you've purchased, slide everything in place, and fasten it all together (see page 120). Make sure each side is level as you position the bed where you want it.

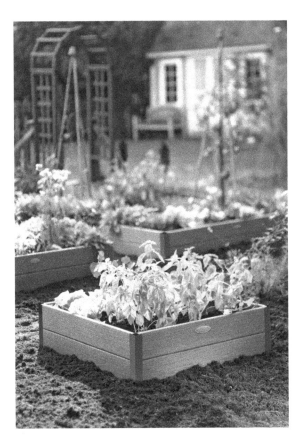

A few packages of corners can allow you to create an instant collection of raised beds with a minimal amount of work. *Gardener's Supply Company*

A Note to New Gardeners Who Have Installed Their First Raised Bed

If your shiny new raised bed is your first foray into gardening, fear not. There are ample online resources that can help a newbie gardener figure out what to plant—or troubleshoot any problems that may arise throughout the growing season.

To help you figure out what seeds to sow or which seedlings to buy at the garden center, think about the items that regularly make it onto your grocery list. Fresh herbs are some of the easiest plants to grow. And they can cost big bucks for a small bunch in the produce aisle. If you love tomatoes, then pick three to five plants that include a nice large slicing tomato and a snack-worthy cherry variety.

Peas, beans, and cucumbers are also relatively easy to grow and yield a sizable harvest; just be sure to give them something to climb.

Even the most experienced gardeners learn through trial and error, so don't be afraid to make mistakes! There's always next year.

Plant the things that most often find themselves in your shopping cart.
© Les Urbainculteurs / Smart Pots

Solutions for Raised Bed Roadblocks

Are there certain limitations holding you back from building a raised bed? Do you lack the necessary tools or skills? Here are some ideas that can help you turn your raised bed aspirations into a reality.

Let someone else do the prep work. Have all your lumber precut where you purchase it, so all you have to worry about is assembly when you get home. Many home centers and some lumberyards offer this service.

Have your materials delivered. If your raised bed materials won't fit in your small car, or if you're limited to public transportation, have them delivered. Better yet, purchase a kit online and receive everything you'll need ready-to-assemble and delivered right to your doorstep.

Borrow or rent tools. If you aspire to build things, but you simply don't own the tools, see if you can borrow them from a friend or neighbor, or rent them. Many home centers feature rental departments where you can pay to reserve and sign out tools for a day or more. Some communities even offer tool libraries where, for a nominal membership fee, you can sign out various tools just as you would a book at the library.

Use what you've got. Not ready to shell out for raised bed materials? Test out your commitment to having a raised bed by raiding your shed, attic, basement, or backyard for items that you can repurpose, such as old washtubs, dressers, or wine crates.

If something is preventing you from building a raised bed, improvise by borrowing tools or arranging for material delivery, etc. *Niki Jabbour*

Consider Drip Irrigation

There are several ways you can give thirsty plants in your raised beds a drink. You could simply fill a watering can and lug it from bed to bed, watering the base of the plants and trying to avoid getting the leaves wet (when water splashes up from the soil and touches the leaves, it can spread diseases to the plant).

Or you can just bring your hose to the beds and water that way—again, gently, at the base of the plants.

But there's a better way to water that requires less effort—it just takes a bit of planning and installation work: drip irrigation.

Drip irrigation is a common method used to water raised beds. It can be installed by a professional or by a keen DIYer. Drip irrigation kits are readily available for purchase at home improvement stores and nurseries. They guide you through the entire installation process and generally come with all the basic parts you'll need to put together a system. There are also add-ons you can purchase later to put your system on a timer or distribute fertilizer.

Drip irrigation is not only efficient, it's a great way to conserve water because it delivers it directly to the root zone of the plants, so no water is lost to evaporation. You're also not watering the weeds. A drip hose is generally looped around the perimeter of the garden and up the middle rows, depending on the width of the garden. You can also have lines going from garden to garden or from pot to pot. The water gently trickles out of what is called an "emitter." Different types of emitters distribute water at different rates (gallons per minute or gallons per hour).

DIY kits

You'll typically find the following components in a DIY drip irrigation kit:

- A Y-shaped connector that connects to the outside faucet. It allows water on one side to feed your regular hose and water on the other side to feed your irrigation system.

- At the very end of the hose, there is a plug, which prevents water from flowing out the end (you only want it to flow out the emitters).

- A pressure regulator to maintain a consistent water pressure.

- A backflow preventer to ensure that nothing is sucked from the garden hose back into your water supply.

- Connectors that allow you to direct irrigation in multiple directions in the garden.

- Tubing or hose that transports the water to the garden.

- Various emitters that release water to the plants a bit differently. They can be referred to as bubblers and xeri emitters. Both emit fine sprays but at different rates. These types of emitters will lose water through wind and evaporation, but they do work around shrubs and trees and in containers.

These are components that are often offered as optional add-ons:

- A drip irrigation standard tubing hole punch allows you to attach a drip line connector to your main hose.

- Timers let you program the start and stop time automatically at the time of day you set it to. They're especially handy if you're away from home frequently.

- Special sensors determine if it's rained and can cancel a timed watering if the soil hasn't yet dried out.

Gardener's Supply Company

Tips from a drip irrigation expert

Brandon Park is the owner of Urban Irrigation Solutions, a company that installs irrigation systems. He says there are a lot of innovative DIY irrigation solutions on the horizon. The trend is moving toward water conservation technologies and better design.

- For raised beds, Park lays driplines on the root system, which he says results in almost zero water loss.

- For new plants that aren't that well established, Park recommends watering every day for about two to three weeks. Once the plants are established, he recommends watering three days a week. The trick is to water plants deeply but less frequently. A heavy soak will provide ample water to the root system and watering less frequently gives it time to dry out before the next soak.

- Every system Park installs has a timer that's set by him or the homeowner to water the raised beds at specific times. Park recommends watering between 5:00 and 7:00 a.m. If you water at night, he warns, the water sits there and

← Driplines running through a raised bed distribute water evenly to the roots. *Ian Wilson*

creates an environment for fungus and bacteria to grow. If you water too late in the morning, you'll lose water to evaporation.

- The type of soil you have is also a big indicator of how frequently you should water, though raised beds that have premium soil should drain well when watered.

- Constant watering throughout the season is naturally going to deplete your soil of nutrients. If you're watering every day, Park recommends fertilizing by adding a fresh layer of soil or manure to your raised beds.

- Park installs a rain sensor for every system, which prevents the garden from being watered when it's not needed.

- While there are DIY irrigation kits, Park says it does take some forethought to design an irrigation system. There is a mathematical formula that determines the size of the pipes needed to ensure water uniformity and pressure. He recommends a homeowner look online for a formula to determine the pressure loss so that everything runs smoothly once it's connected.

- For rooftops, the same systems are used, but the roof must be checked to make sure it has a good water barrier and proper drainage.

- For bigger jobs, an architect will be consulted to check the building's blueprints and make sure the roof is capable of handling soil and the weight of the water.

This irrigation system installed in a raised bed is ready for plants. *Brandon Park*

Concealing drip irrigation It's easiest to conceal hoses and a dripline when the raised beds aren't too far from the hose. Mulch is a good irrigation system cover because it's lightweight and readily available.

Of course, installing an irrigation system sometimes requires digging to run the hoses under a path or section of lawn. This can be done by installing conduit pipe and then running the hose through it to where it needs to go.

Check hoses regularly You'll need to regularly look over your hoses carefully for leaks and for plugged emitters that might have debris in them that prevent the water from coming out where it should.

How Do You Know If You've Overwatered?

Obviously we can't help how much rain Mother Nature decides to give to our plants, but we can control how much we water them. Many plants don't like to be overwatered and will start to show signs of distress if they're getting waterlogged. The soil should dry out completely between watering. Test for moisture by inserting your finger a couple of inches into the soil to see if it feels damp. If it does, don't water. Signs of overwatering include a plant that's wilted and/or has yellow leaves.

An irrigation system is a great way to conserve water, especially when there are multiple beds that need a daily soak. *Steven Biggs*

The Benefits of Mulch

Not only does mulch suppress weeds, it prevents water evaporation and helps soil retain moisture, which means you don't have to water as often. Common mulches include straw, shredded cedar, pine bark, and even compost made from grass clippings, decomposed leaves, and other garden debris.

A layer of straw mulch can keep weeds at bay. It also helps to retain moisture. *Bren Haas*

Chapter 2

Raised Beds for Big Spaces

If you have a yard, you're in luck. You can build one—or two or three or even more— raised beds. You have so many options for different shapes, heights, and sizes. You can experiment with crop rotation.

You can add pathways and trellis systems and irrigation. Nowadays, with the popularity of edible gardening, the choices are endless. There are multiple benefits to growing edibles in raised beds, which have been outlined throughout this book. The first project for this chapter is a plan for what is referred to as the essential raised bed. There are a few different ways to make a raised bed, but this plan in particular has been created to facilitate the addition of various accessories. Because not only are there various design options, there are also many add-ons you can introduce to help you even further with your harvest—pest prevention, staking and trellis systems, frost protection, and more.

Front yard veggie gardens are also becoming more prominent as homeowners eschew the typical expanse of grass for something more practical. Often that's simply where the most sunlight happens to be. So, if your tomatoes are going to ripen in the front and flounder in the back, consider raised beds in your front yard—just be sure to consult your municipality's bylaws before you get started.

If you want to jazz up a raised bed, whether it's visible to the public from the front or side of the house, or you want to add character to the back, there are a few things you can do, including adding a coat of paint or recreating a similar puzzle-like pattern using old pieces of wood in varying hues and thicknesses, as has been done for the upcycled project that can also be found in this chapter (see page 46).

While a raised bed with benches provides a useful, accessible design, setting a pond into a raised bed is an example of taking one's imagination beyond the standard planting scheme.

For further inspiration, you may discover that many community garden plots have adopted the neat and tidy aesthetic of raised beds. Botanical gardens and other public spaces dedicated to growing food can also be great sources of ideas.

The Essential Raised Bed

Design adapted by Scott McKinnon
Photography by *Donna Griffith*
Illustration by Len Churchill

If your beds are going in the backyard—or a community garden space—then you might be content with a typical, easy-to-construct design. There are a few easy ways to make your standard, rectangular raised bed. One is simply to stack timber, tailored to the width and length of your space, staggering the corner joints and securing with 6-inch nails driven down from each top corner through ³⁄₁₆-inch pilot holes. Another way is to cut two 8-foot 1-inch by 6-inch boards in half for the ends, and use four 1 by 6-inch boards for the two longer sides, stacking them two high and attaching everything with outdoor screws to four by four posts positioned on the inside corners. Be sure to leave a few inches on the ends of the posts to anchor the raised beds firmly into the ground. (And refer to step 6 for an important tip about reinforcing the sides.)

Tools

- Tape measure
- Hammer
- Circular saw
- Carpenter's square
- Rubber mallet or hand sledgehammer
- Level
- Reciprocating saw or handsaw
- Drill with countersink bit and ³⁄₁₆" twist bit
- Eye and ear protection
- Work gloves

Materials

- 3½" and 1¼" deck screws
- (2) 2 × 10" × 10'
- (1) 4 × 4" × 8' (or 2 × 4") (for stakes)
- (3) 2 × 4 × 8'
- (1) 2 × 2" or use scrap from a 2 × 4" sawn in half

Cut list

PART	DIMENSION	PCS
Frame, side pieces	1½ × 9¼ × 45"	2
Frame, long pieces	1½ × 9¼ × 72"	2
Corner posts	3½ × 3½ × 24"	4
Top rails, long sides (from 45° mitered ends)	1½ × 3½ × 68½"	2
Top rails, short sides (from 45° mitered ends)	1½ × 3½ × 44½"	2
Stakes	1½ × 1½ × 12"	2

45° mitre

long edge top rail

short edge top rail

midpoint stake

frame side

corner posts

frame end

top rail

¼"

frame side/end

72"

SIDE VIEW

45"

END VIEW

continued

How to Make the Essential Raised Bed

1. Cut pieces to size.

With a circular saw, cut a 45-inch and a 72-inch piece out of each 2 × 10-inch × 10-foot board. Use a carpenter's square to make sure the cuts are straight and at 90 degrees. These are your frame pieces.

2. Create the frame.

Line up the side pieces on the outside of the ends (the shorter pieces inside the longer ones). Make sure everything is flush, and drill three evenly spaced pilot holes through the sides and end pieces at each corner. Use 3½-inch deck screws to fasten everything together.

3. Make the corner posts.

Cut the 4 × 4-inch × 8-foot board equally into four pieces (about 24 inches each). Trim the ends of each post into a point, using a reciprocating saw or handsaw. This will make it easier to drive them into the ground.

4. Position the frame.

Remove any grass or weeds that will end up beneath your raised bed. Make sure the ground is level. Once you're ready, place the raised bed frame in its final destination. Measure diagonally between the opposing corners to ensure the bed is square. Measurements should be equal on both diagonals.

5. Secure the frame.

In each inside corner, position the corner posts and use a mallet or hand sledge and a wood block to drive the post into the ground. The tops should be about 2 inches below the top of the bed frame. Check that the frame is sitting level. Once it's in place, drill pilot holes from the outside into the post and secure with 3½-inch deck screws.

6. Reinforce the midpoint.

Using a mallet, strike a 2 × 4 stake firmly into the ground on the outside of the bed frame at the midpoint. Do this for each long side (don't worry about the ends), and secure with a couple of screws. You could also use rebar. This is an important step; it will prevent the lumber from shifting over time.

7. Install the top rail.

Out of an 8-foot board, cut a 45-degree miter close to one end. Measure 68½ inches from the shorter end of the miter, and cut an opposing miter at that point. Repeat with a second 8-foot piece.

Out of the remaining piece, cut two pieces the same way but 44½ inches between the miters.

Secure with 1¼-inch screws, making sure that there's an even overlap all around. The boards should overlap the inside edge of the frame walls by ¼ inch all around.

continued

Plant It!

Arriving at your local garden center can be extremely overwhelming—especially if you go without a list. Your first visit may simply be a reconnaissance mission where you scope out what's available. Then when you get home, you can figure out what to plant in your raised bed. Essentially, you want to plant your grocery list, with tried-and-true family favorites and a few new-to-you edibles planted somewhere in the mix.

Think about the foods that you frequently use when cooking. Are you constantly throwing a packet of fresh herbs in your cart? Those add up; it's much cheaper to buy one plant and snip it throughout the season. If it's an herb you really like, buy a backup plant—or two—just in case you give one plant too much of a haircut.

Keep in mind that side dish mainstays, like carrots and potatoes, can be stored over the winter months. And an overabundance of cucumbers can keep you in pickles until spring.

What do you generally toss into a salad? Add to your list green onions, tomatoes, and a variety of greens, from lettuces to kale and mustard.

The key is to plant a variety of food that your family will enjoy throughout the harvest season—and, if you think ahead, until the end of the winter.

Plant New-To-You Edibles in Your Raised Bed

Besides your dependable list of edibles that you enjoy, try to add at least one that's new to you each season. It's fun to discover new flavors for meals and preserving. And it's entertaining to serve uncommon-looking edibles and explain to your guests what they are. Here are a few that you may encounter as you flip through seed catalogs.

Lemongrass, which looks like a dracaena, can usually be found among the herbs. Its fragrant stalks can be used in everything from herbal tea to Thai cooking.

Accessorize Your Raised Bed

So you've built a basic raised bed. What now? Just like a car, raised beds aren't one-size-fits-all. Some gardeners may need a few extra features, like pest preventers or season extenders, while others will benefit from some helpful modifications such as extra drainage allowances. Here are a few ideas that you can use to customize your own raised bed.

Line your bed with landscape fabric.

Depending on where you place your new raised bed, lining the bottom with landscape fabric will prevent weeds from growing up into your pristine soil. It can be found by the roll at home improvement centers and hardware stores. The fabric is permeable, so water drains through it. It's also a great material to lay under the pathways of gravel or mulch that you may create between your raised beds to thwart weeds.

To make it easier to toss the new soil into the bed, you may want to first secure the landscape cloth to the bottom sides of your raised bed using stainless-steel staples. *Donna Griffith*

Keep voles and moles out with hardware cloth.

The term hardware cloth can be a bit deceiving because this material is not made of fabric. In fact, it's more of a sturdy wire mesh—like chicken wire, but with smaller holes—that will keep digging rodents, such as moles, voles, and gophers, from coming up into your beds to eat your harvest from below. Lay the hardware cloth at the bottom of a raised bed before you add the landscape fabric. Be sure to wear gloves for this task because the ends are very sharp. Use tin snips to cut a piece to size, and make sure you secure it firmly at the bottom of the bed with stainless-steel staples. *Andrea Hungerford*

Deter slugs with copper tape.

If slugs happen to be a problem in the garden, there are copper slug tapes on the market that are meant to repel them. Copper is said to contain a small electrical charge that keeps slugs and snails from crossing over it. Place it around a raised bed and challenge those annoying insects to dare to come to the other side. *Donna Griffith*

Turn Your Raised Bed Into a Mini Hoop House

Start your season early or extend it well into fall by covering your raised bed with row cover. Row cover comes in different weights depending on the season in which you use it. It can help protect your crops from the elements and pests.

Tools

- Utility knife blade or PEX pipe cutter
- 6 to 12 spring clamps
- Eye protection
- Work gloves

Materials

- ½" PEX pipe (5 pieces cut to 75")
- Plastic or row cover (8 × 14')
- (10) ½" PVC conduit clamps

1: Attach ½" PVC conduit clamps with screws every few inches along the length of your raised bed on the inside (in this case, they're screwed to the top rail, as shown in the Essential Raised Bed plan, page 38). Make sure they're the same distance apart on both sides so the PEX hoops line up.

Cut your lengths of PEX pipe using a utility knife blade or PEX pipe cutter. *Donna Griffith*

2: Bend and place the PEX through the clamps on each side to form a hoop shape. *Donna Griffith*

Note: If you're concerned about snow load, you may want to create a spine from another length of PEX that's attached down the middle of your hoops. Attach this with 1¾-inch #8 stainless-steel machine bolts and wingnuts (for easy disassembly).

3: When you're ready to add a row cover, netting, or plastic, drape the material over the cover frame, centering it from side to side and end to end. Use the clamps to attach the material to the rail so it doesn't blow away. To prevent plastic covers from overheating your crops, you can roll up the ends and clamp the material to the outside ribs to let the air flow through. *Tara Nolan*

INSTALL STAKES AND TRELLISES.
It's very important to stake plants to keep leaves and stems from touching the ground (which can encourage disease) and from crowding out other plants in the garden. Try to add any cages, stakes, or trellises close to the time of planting because stems can inadvertently be snapped if you try to add them later to a more mature plant. Staking plants also frees up space in the garden for other plants. If climbers head upward, all of a sudden you have new real estate.

If you need to tie stems and branches to a stake, use a gentle material, like a Velcro plant tie, so that you don't inadvertently harm the plant. *Brenda Franklin*

DEER-PROOF YOUR BED.
Deer are a little harder to deter than smaller animals, but there are ways to keep them out of your raised beds. The structures are just built on a larger scale. Fencing in an area at a height where the deer cannot leap over will help, but you can also create fencing that simply fits over a raised bed. Some gardeners also cover the top of a raised bed with fencing, and simply lift off the "lid" when they want to get into the garden. *Meighan Makarchuk*

INSTALL AN IRRIGATION SYSTEM.
If you travel or you're away from your garden frequently, an irrigation system will keep the plants in your raised beds well hydrated so you can still come home to a healthy crop—and hopefully edibles that are ready to harvest. (See Chapter 1, page 30, for more information.) *Hilary Dahl for Seattle Urban Farm Co.*

ADD DRAINAGE.
It's important that your raised beds drain well so that the roots of the plants are able to dry out between watering and to prevent them from drowning in water that won't drain. If you're placing your raised bed in an area of the yard that does not tend to dry out after heavy watering, you can add a layer of crushed gravel to the bottom before you add in the soil. Some beds also can benefit from weep holes, which are holes drilled upward through the sides of the bed that allow water to drain.

MEASURE TEMPERATURES WITH AN INDOOR/OUTDOOR THERMOMETER.
Believe it or not, even in the dead of winter, the solar energy captured by a cold frame can make it too hot inside for your plants. A min/max thermometer will help you determine whether or not you need to vent your cold frame (which is done simply by opening the lid and using a sturdy stake to keep it lifted). Keep in mind that with the lid closed, you don't want the temperatures inside to rise above 60°F during the day. *Tara Nolan*

Raised Bed with Upcycled Wood

Designed by Scott McKinnon
Photography by Donna Griffith
Illustration by Len Churchill

This project design takes the standard raised bed to a whole new level. Old strips of wood in varying grains, colors, and thicknesses have been used to create an eye-catching garden. Let's call it rustic-chic.

The snazzy raised bed shown here was built for the side yard of a corner lot and has attracted many appreciative glances from the neighbors and dog walkers who happen by. It also happens to be in a prime, sunny spot where veggies don't just thrive, they're almost busting out of the bed! Besides using good-quality soil, where you place your bed is one of the key ingredients to reaping a bountiful harvest. You want to make sure the space you choose sees at least six to eight hours of sun a day, especially if you're planting heat-loving edibles like peppers and tomatoes.

To create the look, strips of wood are sourced from a variety of different places and cut to different lengths. These strips are then carefully pieced over panels made from cedar fence boards. They kind of act like a protective barrier, potentially prolonging the life of your bed. This effect could be used on any size of raised bed—even ones that have already been built, if you want to jazz them up a little.

Scott McKinnon, the project's designer and builder, is always on the lookout for old pallets, fence boards, and barn boards. He's been known to make special trips to a location if he hears that something good is up for grabs. "Anything with a patina," he says. A visit to McKinnon's workshop reveals his talent for upcycling old wood that's made its way onto the back of his pickup truck and into new projects for the home.

Once you've got a selection of different types of wood, you can get started laying everything out. It takes a bit of patience and work to piece everything together for the cool effect shown here, but this "puzzle" is ultimately worth it.

Tools

- Hammer
- Miter saw
- Cordless circular saw or a dozuki handsaw (we used a Silky woodboy)
- Eye and ear protection
- Work gloves

Materials

- (9) 2 × 3½" × 6' cedar fence boards
- (6) 2 × 2" × 30" spruce garden stakes (or create your own)
- Old strips of pallet wood (enough to cover the planter, approximately 30 sq. ft.)
- 1¼" finishing nails (if you're not using a pneumatic nailer)
- 1½" brass screws

Cut list

PART	DIMENSION	PCS
End panels	3½" × 3' (height × length)	6
Long panels	3½" × 6' (height × length)	6

long side panels

2¼" to 2½"

short end panels

garden "stake"
corner post

random length pallet wood strips

72"

10½"

30"

continued

How to Make a Raised Bed with Upcycled Wood

1. Prepare the long panels.

Cut three cedar fence boards in half, leaving six pieces 3 feet long. (These will be used to make the end panels. Set them aside for now.) To create the long panels, lay three 6-foot boards parallel and pushed together. Lifting the ends of the three boards together, slide a stake under the edges flush with the board ends and the flat end flush at the top. Attach with two screws per board. Attach another stake to support the center of the panel. Create the other panel in the same way with the last three 6-foot boards and stakes.

2. Cut out different lengths and types of wood.

Use a dozuki saw or a cordless circular saw to make quick trims here and there so you can work out the whole puzzle. Try not to place the seams close to each other. This will create a more randomized pattern. Be sure to leave some overhang at the ends, which will cover the short panels when you're putting together the whole raised bed.

3. Figure out your pattern.

From your selection of old wood—pallet strips, old barn board, and so on—start to lay out a random pattern to cover one of these long panels. Choose different thicknesses and wood hues.

4. Secure the puzzle pieces.

Use small finishing nails or a pneumatic nailer to attach the boards to the panels.

5. Make the end panels.

Lay out three of the 3-foot boards. Place the stakes underneath as you did for the long panels, but for these, do not place them flush at the ends. Measure in 2¼ to 2½ inches, and nail the edge of the stakes. This means in each corner you'll have the two stakes meeting when the bed comes together. Repeat for the other side panel. You can now lay out a puzzle on these pieces as well.

With the stakes pointing up, assemble the four panels together and fasten with the screws. Trim the edges that you have left so that the corners are flush.

6. Place the container in its new home.

Move the raised bed to the desired location; use a large mallet or sledgehammer to drive the stakes into the ground.

7. Level and square as required.

Use the stakes to lift the bed's corners up and down to eventually square the entire bed. Fill in the spaces with soil. Lay mulch around the outside of the bed to finish off the area.

You're now ready to fill the bed with soil and plant!

Raised Bed with Benches

Designed by Chris Hill for Bonnie Plants
Photography by Donna Griffith
Illustration by Len Churchill, based on Bonnie Plants plans

This garden may look complicated to build because it's so impressive-looking, but the steps are quite simple and streamlined—especially if you have your materials precut at a home improvement store.

Raised beds are also useful when the ground beneath them is compact, making it almost impossible to dig a regular garden into the ground. In this case, the raised bed is covering a mess of roots from an old bush (that had previously been removed) that were hard to dig up from the compacted earth. Before soil was added, hardware cloth was laid across the bottom, followed by a layer of landscape fabric. As a result of the depth, triple mix from a reputable soil company was used to fill a great deal of the bed, with a layer of compost dug into the top. Because of the height of this bed, make sure the area beneath will drain well as the soil dries out.

Tools

- Miter saw or circular saw
- Drill/driver
- Clamps
- Carpenter's square
- Tape measure
- Eye and ear protection
- Work gloves

Materials

- (1) 2 × 2" × 8' board
- (3) 2 × 4" × 8' boards
- (8) 2 × 6" × 8' boards
- (2) 2" × 8" × 8' boards
- (3) 1-lb. boxes 2½" deck screws
- (1) 1-lb. box 3" deck screws

Cut list

PART	DIMENSION	PCS
Side slats	1½ × 5½ × 45"	8
Bottom side slats	1½ × 7¼ × 45"	4
Inner posts	1½ × 3½ × 14"	8
Bracket supports	1½ × 5½ × 16"	4
Brackets	1½ × 5½ × 15½"	8
Outer posts	1½ × 3½ × 16½"	4
Seat slats	1½ × 5½ × 24"	8
Seat cleats	1½ × 1½ × 20½"	4

seat slats

seat cleat

inner posts

outer post

side slats

bottom side slat

brackets

bracket
support

seat slats

1½"

13½"

6¼"   4¾"   1¾"

4"

SIDE VIEW

5½"   5½"

45°   45°

15½"

SEAT BRACKET

45"   45"

TOP VIEW

continued

How to Make a Raised Bed with Benches

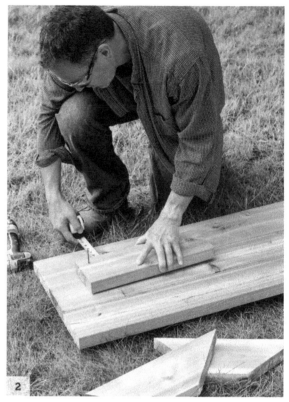

1. Make the side assemblies.

Create each side assembly by positioning two side slats and a bottom side slat with the ends flush. Attach the inner posts 13½ inches from the ends and 1¾ inches from the edge of the bottom side slat. Use 2½-inch deck screws to fasten. Repeat to create three more assemblies, using two side slats, one bottom side slat, and two inner posts for each. Divide the four assemblies into two sets of two.

2. Add the bracket supports for the bench.

Attach a bracket support to the opposite side of each assembly, overlapping the two side slats that will be closest to the top. Fasten in place with 2½-inch deck screws.

3. Connect the brackets.

Attach the brackets to both the bracket support and the side slats with 2½-inch deck screws.

4. Join the seat cleat.

Place the seat cleat flush with the brackets, and attach it to the side slats with 2½-inch deck screws.

5. Add the seat slats.

Set the first seat slat in place and attach it to both the cleat and the brackets with 2½-inch deck screws.

6. Attach the second seat slat.

Using a ¼-inch scrap piece of wood as a spacer, set the second seat slat in place and attach it to the brackets. Then remove the spacer.

continued

7. Join the outer posts.

Attach an outer post to the sides of two of the side assemblies. It should be placed on the outside with half covering the wood and half overlapping.

8. Join together the first set of side assemblies.

Attach one assembly with the outer post to another, making sure the ends of the side assemblies sit flush with the outer posts. Fasten with 3-inch deck screws. Place in the garden where you want the raised bed to go.

9. Fit all the sides together.

Attach the remaining side assemblies with 3-inch deck screws. They should fit together snugly, like a puzzle.

Succession Planting in Raised Beds

With raised beds, you don't have to limit your growing period to one season. You can plant cool-weather crops, like peas and broccoli, in the spring, heat-seekers, like tomatoes and peppers, for a summer harvest, and so on. When one crop comes out, another can be waiting in the wings (or under your grow lights), ready to be dug in. It takes a little bit of planning, but succession planting is the key to a continuous, fruitful harvest from early spring right up until the snow flies.

One way to keep track of everything is to keep a list of early-, mid-, and late-season crops that you want to plant so that you know what is maturing when.

Many only consider using their grow lights in the winter to produce spring seedlings.

However, a grow light system is a great tool for more advanced green thumbs who want to keep producing high-quality seedlings for summer and autumn succession planting.

You can also stagger succession planting. For example, if you're sowing lettuce seeds, rather than planting them all at once, sow them a few days apart so that as you're harvesting one row, another is filling in. You can do this with lots of different crops, from root veggies to climbing edibles, such as peas and beans.

ABOVE: Grow lights can help you get a head start on crops. *Niki Jabbour*

LEFT: Once the lettuce started to bolt in these raised beds, it was removed to make way for a new crop. *Paul Zammit*

Utility Raised Bed

If aesthetics are not an issue, then this no-frills, functional raised bed may be just what you need to grow a high volume of produce. This bed is considerably longer than any of the other projects in this section, but it's 5 feet wide. This should still make it accessible to weed and plant by reaching in from the outside. Big beds like this one are great for crops where you want to plant a lot of one variety, like corn or pickling cucumbers. This project also provides a lesson in how to reinforce the sides. Many raised beds are made from stacked boards secured in the corners, but on the long ends they can curve inward or outward over time. Tie rods have been used here to provide plenty of support and keep beds square.

Tools

- Circular saw or sliding miter saw
- Drill
- Countersink bit
- ½" spade bit
- Wrench
- Shovel
- Eye and ear protection
- Work gloves

Cut list

PART	DIMENSION	PCS
Side	1½ × 5½" × 16'	6
End	1½ × 5½" × 5'	6
Braces	1½ × 5½" × 15'	12

Materials

- (8) 2 × 6" × 16' cedar
- (1) 2 × 6" × 8' (for braces)
- (4) ½" × 6' galvanized tie rods with washers and bolts
- (5 lbs.) 2½" deck screws

How to Make the Utility Raised Bed

1. Build the frame.

Start by screwing together the first level (sides to ends), predrilling the holes with a countersink bit so you don't split the ends. After the first level is done, attach vertical 2 × 6 braces at the inside corners. Add the next layer of sides and ends, alternating the lengths to make the corners a little tighter and more interesting-looking. The sides and ends are all equal lengths, so adjoining corners are alternated in opposite ways, and the overall size of the raised bed is 5 × 16 feet. Attach more vertical 2 × 6 braces every 4 or 5 feet on the inside of the boards.

2. Brace the frame.

A long raised bed built from 2 × 6s needs to be held together at the center or it will bow out from the weight of the dirt. Add a 2 × 6 vertical support and drill two ½-inch-diameter holes at the same points on both sides.

Push galvanized, threaded tie rods through the holes, and then thread galvanized washers and nuts over the ends. Tighten until the distance at the center and the ends is the same. Threaded tie rods are zinc-plated, usually ⅜, ½, or ⅝ inch in diameter, that are tapped with threads over the entire length. If gaps eventually appear at the corners, dig out some of the adjoining soil to reduce the pressure, push the walls back together as best you can, and reinforce the corners with large metal angles. Trim off any protruding hardware.

TIP

A center divider could also be created out of wood.

Other Ways to Build Raised Beds

When it comes to raised bed design, there are so many avenues you can take. Some might be trickier than others to execute, so if you're building a raised bed yourself, opt for a simpler design for your first one. That way you can get planting sooner!

You can be as creative as you like, or simply opt for a utilitarian look that gets the job done. The end result—fresh, homegrown produce—will be the same no matter what your raised bed happens to look like. Here are a few other easy and more complicated construction ideas.

Finials, paint, and levels make for a visually interesting raised bed.

"Having logs slowly breaking down is excellent for biodiversity!" says James, who advises that you never move wood beyond a quarantine zone if it has been infected by an invasive pest. *Sean James*

When life gives you lemons, build a raised bed

A multitude of tree trunks felled by an incredibly destructive pest. What do you do? "For those who are looking to save a buck or who are more into a freestyle design, an inexpensive way to create a raised bed is to use waste wood in place of timbers," says landscape designer Sean James, whose company, Fern Ridge Landscaping, put these beds together. "These ash logs were taken down as a result of the invasive emerald ash borer, but they've found new life as a garden," he says. In this case, there was no construction work necessary. Logs were simply laid in a raised bed shape and the area was filled accordingly with soil.

Stack timbers into a raised bed

Perhaps the easiest way to build a raised bed that doesn't really require much woodworking know-how is to stack timbers and stagger the end joints—like you'd see with a log cabin. To fasten everything together, hammer landscape spikes into all four corners and, voilà, a raised bed.

Piling rocks and bricks

If you have a pile of old interlocking brick or rocks that don't yet have a purpose in your garden, stack them to create a raised bed. If possible, try to stagger each piece to add more stability to your structure.

This brand new raised bed was built from timbers. *Bren Haas*

Though timber raised beds look polished and new when they're first built, over time they will age to a nice faded patina. *Bren Haas*

If you don't happen to have a neglected pile, check out a site such as Craigslist to see if someone in your area happens to be giving materials away. *Sean James*

Weave a raised bed from wattle

Wattle is a term used to describe a technique for weaving a fence or structure from twigs and sticks around stakes. You need to use young wood that will bend easily as you weave it in and out of the stakes. Weed trees are great for this because you don't need to worry about sacrificing a good tree in the name of garden art. This technique used to be popular for building fences that would contain livestock, but nowadays it's more of a decorative feature. Think of the side of a basket.

Wattling is also a great technique for building decorative plant supports.

Wattle makes for a gorgeous, rustic-looking raised bed.

Protect the sides of the bed with plastic to avoid rot. Cable ties can be used to fasten the sides together. *Niki Jabbour*

Enclose a raised bed with concrete blocks

Concrete blocks are like ready-made walls for your raised bed. There's no woodworking or assembly involved; you simply outline the area where you'd like a raised bed, make sure it's level, and then line 'em up! You even get a bonus growing area—fill the block holes with the same healthy soil you used to fill your bed, and fill those with plants too. If you want the border to be more decorative, fill the holes with drought-tolerant sedum or other low-maintenance plants.

Be careful not to use cinder blocks, which look the same as concrete blocks, especially if you're growing food, because they may contain fly ash, a harmful contaminant. *Amy Andrychowicz*

Build a straw bale bed

A straw bale garden, a concept made popular by author and gardener Joel Karsten, is another type of raised bed. Straw bales can be used to outline a temporary raised bed, or you can actually use them as a raised bed by planting right into the bale itself. Just be sure to use straw rather than hay because hay can contain unwanted seeds that will root in your garden.

Make a raised bed with half-lap joints

For experienced woodworkers, making a half-lap joint is a great technique that can be applied to a raised bed design. Basically, you're stacking T- and upside-down-T-shaped wood with half of the corners cut out. Not only does this make the bed stronger, it also makes for a visually interesting raised bed. (Half-lap joints were also used to strengthen the structure that became the greenhouse on page 100.)

Any square-edged timber can be used to make a half-lap joint—4 × 4, 4 × 6, 6 × 6, and so on—which is essentially notching out exactly half of the thickness (or depth) for each piece that will be matched together. A thickness planer can be used to ensure each piece of wood has the exact same dimensions before you get started.

Cutting half-lap joints

Lay out and stack your wood so that the most flattering sides will be facing outward. Mark whether the pieces will be cut from the top or the bottom.

Choose your pieces of wood, and place the flattest side of each one face-down on a work surface. Mark the wood 3½ inches from the end, and use a ruler to draw a straight line. Set the cutting depth of your circular saw to 1¾ inches, and cut along the 3½-inch end. Repeat this step until you have a series of parallel cuts that are about ¼ inch apart (photo A). These are called "kerf cuts." Use a hammer or a mallet to chip away at the cut pieces (photo B). Clean up the area with a wood chisel because you want the boards to rest flat when you stack them.

Once all of your half-lap joints have been cut, test-fit all the corners by restacking the raised bed and then attach.

A

B

Weld a raised bed out of metal: If you'd like to hire a professional welder, steel makes for a durable raised bed. It also develops a lovely rust-colored patina over time. Orchard People

Chapter 3

Raised Beds for Small Spaces

Who says you can't have a vegetable garden if you happen to have a tiny space? Be it a balcony, a rooftop patio, or a small urban yard, if you're lucky enough to have sunlight, your green thumb just needs to get a little creative.

Of course there are unique challenges, such as strong wind gusts if you're high up. But a few tricks here and there will help to customize your space according to the conditions presented by the chosen space for your garden. And this doesn't just mean a few herbs and a couple of tomatoes. You can grow root vegetables and cucumbers and even melons in a small area.

Just a few square feet can support a raised bed that will provide a bounty of fresh produce. The increasing popularity of vertical gardening means there are also lots of kits available to consumers now that will help support dreams of a harvest, even high up.

The ideas in this section include getting creative with vintage finds and giving them a modern spin, discovering ready-made kits and applying a tiered approach to the typical idea of what a raised bed is.

As for what you can grow? Well, pretty much anything—within reason. When it comes to tomatoes, for example, opt for bushy, dwarf varieties that are more compact. Choose mini versions of pumpkins instead of the ones that will win medals for their girth at fall fairs. And for vining plants like cucumbers, think about growing up rather than out. If not enough sun is an issue, you may not be able to grow the heat-seekers like peppers, but you just might have a thriving mini plot full of beans and greens, including lettuce and spinach.

As with a large space, trial and error will help you determine what will grow best in the small space that you have.

Vertical Herb (or Lettuce) Planter

Designed by Chris Hill for Bonnie Plants
Photography by Donna Griffith
Illustration by Len Churchill, based on Bonnie Plants plans

What's the solution for a small, compact area where you want to grow food, but don't believe you have the space? Grow up! Vertical gardening has become popular in urban areas where outdoor expanses can be rather limited. This planter allows for a very thorough variety of herbs to be planted that you can enjoy in summer meals—basil, dill, oregano, chives, and more. Lettuce would do equally well in this vertical raised bed—you can basically grow a whole salad bar right outside your door. You just need at least six to eight hours of sunlight in your small space per day in order for your edibles to flourish.

Tools

- Miter saw or circular saw
- Drill/driver
- Clamps
- Carpenter's square
- Tape measure
- Eye and ear protection
- Work gloves

Materials

- (1) 1 × 2" × 8' board
- (1) 1 × 4" × 8' board
- (2) 1 × 6" × 8' boards
- (6) 1 × 6" × 8' tongue-and-groove boards
- (2) 1 × 8" × 8' boards
- (1) 2 × 4" × 8' board
- (2) 2 × 10" × 10' boards
- (68) 1¼" deck screws
- (18) 2½" deck screws
- Sealer (optional)

Cut list

PART	DIMENSION	PCS
Legs	1½ × 9¼ × 59¼"	4
Leg braces (see illustration for special cuts)	1½ × 3½ × 23"	2
Leg brace supports (see illustration for special cuts)	¾ × 3½ × 19"	2
Cleats	¾ × 1½ × 5½"	14
Back slats	⅝ × 5½ × 50"	6
Back supports	¾ × 5½ × 33½"	3
Bottom support	1 ½ × 3½ × 30½"	1
Top shelf	¾ × 5½ × 30½"	1
Shelves	¾ × 7¼ × 30½"	6

top shelf

tongue-in-groove
back slats

back supports

1½"

cleats

legs

shelves

leg brace
support

bottom
support

drain holes

cleats

leg brace

5⅝"

11⅜"

6"

SIDE VIEW

⅞"
45°
⅞"
⅞"
⅞"
45°
15/16"
23"
15°
15°
LEG BRACE

15/16"
15°
19"
LEG BRACE SUPPORT

2¾"
7 3/16"
8"
8"
8"
8"
6 9/16"
2½"
45°
2¾"
1⅞"
2¾"
15°
15°
1¾"
7 3/16"
8"
8"
8"
8"
10½"
59¼"
LEG

continued

How to Make a Vertical Herb Planter

1. Prepare the leg assemblies.

Attach the cleats to the inside of the legs. These will be used to support the shelves.

2. Create the frame.

The end assemblies are braced A-frames made from natural cedar. Make the leg assemblies by cutting the 2 × 10s, lining up the ends, and attaching with screws.

3. Create the leg supports.

Lay out and cut the ends of the leg brace support and leg brace according to the illustration on page 67. Attach with 2½-inch screws on the inside and 1¼-inch screws on the outside.

Attach the bottom support to the leg assemblies.

4. Assemble the back slats.

Fit the back slats together to create a solid panel. After fitting the back slats, measure the width of the panel to make sure you have the proper overhang on the back supports.

Attach the three back supports to the back slats.

5. Fasten the back slats to the legs.

Set the back assembly in place between the leg assemblies and flush against the bottom support, and attach.

6. Add drainage holes.

Drill drain holes in the bottom support in line with the grooves in the back slats.

7. Secure the top and bottom shelves.

Attach the top shelf to the top cleats using 1¼-inch screws.

8. Slide in the shelves over the cleats.

Place the bottom shelf on the bottom cleats, and start adding the first layer of soil. Insert the next shelf on the cleats and add the next layer of soil. Continue adding shelves and soil to the rest of the planter. Adjust the shelves to allow the soil to cascade down to the level below. Manipulate the soil on each level as you plant. You'll need to make several adjustments during this process. Make sure the soil continues to cascade down until it's set in place. Place two to three plants on each level for the best results. Water the base of the plants thoroughly, making sure to limit the amount of water that falls directly onto the leaves of the plants. Applying a sealer to the bottom of the leg braces will help to limit moisture-wicking.

Elevated Planter Box

Designed by (and kit and step-by-steps
provided by) Freedom Growing
Photography by Donna Griffith

With the rising popularity of raised beds,
companies are coming up with easy-to-assemble
kits that don't require many tools or a ton of
woodworking expertise. Materials generally come
pre-cut with detailed step-by-step instructions,
depending on the project. This one, designed by a
company called Freedom Growing, uses galvanized,
powder-coated steel to create a sturdy base into
which cedar boards are placed and then attached by
stainless-steel bolts.

This Elevated Planter Box model comes in a variety
of eye-catching colors that make it a conversation
piece before you've even added the plants.

While having a kit mailed to your home is
convenient, be sure to look into what the shipping
charges will be. A quick online search will reveal
companies that may be creating raised bed kits
in your area, meaning you can arrange for a local
delivery or even pick it up yourself. Local nurseries
or home-improvement stores may offer ready-to-
make kits as well.

Tools

- Phillips screwdriver
- ⁷⁄₁₆" ratcheting socket wrench
- Eye protection
- Work gloves

Materials

(All the following are included with the kit)
- 4 long rails
- 4 legs
- 4 short rails
- (32) ½" carriage bolts
- (32) 1" carriage bolts
- (32) lock washers
- (32) flat washers
- (64) nuts
- (2) long cedar boards
- (2) long cedar boards with rounded edge
- (2) short cedar boards
- (2) short cedar boards with rounded edge
- (6) slats
- (1) 2 × 4" center support beam
- (1) piece of lining material

How to Make an Elevated Planter Box

Metal frame assembly

1. Unpack and start with the leg assemblies.

Unpack all parts onto a soft surface to prevent marking of powder-coated finish on the product. For this project, landscape fabric was used to keep all the pieces safe. All steps are to be hand-tightened until all the parts are in place.

Lay one long rail on a soft surface with the channel facing up. Lay two of the legs flat on the ground on either side of the long rail. Slide the bottom of the leg underneath the long rail, matching up the hole patterns on each end of the long rail. (To tell the difference between the top and bottom of the leg, the ½-inch bends in the leg are close to the bottom.)

Attach the long rail to the inside of the bottom of the leg with a ½-inch carriage bolt, through the holes of the legs and long rails. Secure the bolt with a lock washer and nut per hole. Make sure the nut and washer sit inside the channel with the bolt head on the outside of the leg. Hand-tighten.

2. Add the remaining rails.

Lay another long rail on the same legs just above the ½-inch bend of the leg, matching up the hole patterns. Attach the long rail to the inside of the legs by inserting a ½-inch carriage bolt, through the holes of both the leg and long rail. Secure the bolt with a one-lock washer and one nut per hole. Make sure the nut and washer sit inside the channel with the bolt head on the outside of the leg. Hand-tighten, and set aside the assembly.

Repeat the previous steps using the remaining legs and long rails.

continued

3. Fasten the short rails.

While one of the assemblies from above is still laying down, match the hole pattern on the bottom of the leg with a short rail, so the short rail is standing straight up in the air with the channel facing inward. Attach the short rails to the inside of the leg by inserting a ½-inch carriage bolt through the predrilled holes and securing the bolt with one lock washer and one nut per each hole; there are two holes. Make sure the nut and washer sit inside the channel with the bolt head on the outside of the leg. Hand-tighten until all of the rails are attached. Now repeat this process on the other leg.

Stand up another short rail on the same legs just above the ½-inch bend of the leg, matching up the hole patterns. Attach the short rails to the inside of the center of the legs by inserting a ½-inch carriage bolt through the predrilled holes and securing the bolt with one lock washer and one nut per hole; there are two holes per leg. Make sure the nut and washer sit inside the channel with the bolt head on the outside of the leg. Hand-tighten until all of the rails are attached. Repeat this process on the other leg.

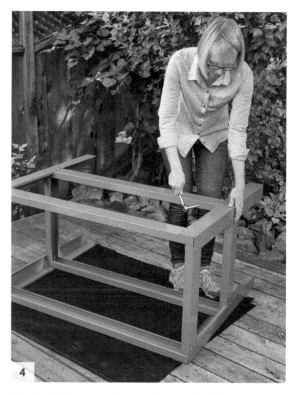

4. Add the finishing touches to the frame.

To complete the metal frame, match up the hole patterns of both halves of the legs and rails, and attach the pieces together by inserting ½-inch carriage bolts through the predrilled holes and securing the bolts with one lock washer and one nut per hole. Make sure the nut and washer sit inside the channel with the bolt head on the outside of the leg. Once all of the bolts and nuts are in place, tighten all of the nuts and bolts using the ⁷⁄₁₆-inch ratcheting socket wrench, making sure the bolt heads sit flush on the legs. Be careful to not over-tighten.

Place the 2 × 4 center support beam into the center of the top short rails. Do this by putting the 2 × 4 in horizontally and twisting it so the slots cut in the beam fit snuggly on the bends of the short rails.

Wood box assembly

1. Fit the boards in place.

With the frame right-side up, place the long cedar boards with predrilled holes on the long sides of the frame, making sure the countersunk holes face inside the box. Match up the pre-drilled holes with the square holes in the steel frame, and attach the wood to the metal frame using the 1-inch carriage bolts, flat washer, and nut. Make sure the carriage bolt head is on the outside of the frame and the washer and nut are on the inside of the box. Repeat on the other side. Tighten all of the nuts and bolts using the ⁷⁄₁₆-inch ratcheting socket wrench. Do not over-tighten or you may split the cedar.

(Hint: If the holes are not lining up, flip over the boards or try it on the other side. Or put the tip of a screwdriver in the holes and wiggle it around until the holes line up. Make sure the square shaft of the carriage bolt sits flush inside the square hole of the steel frame.)

Place the short cedar boards with predrilled holes on the end of the frame, making sure the countersunk holes face inside the box. Match up the predrilled holes with the square holes in the steel frame, and attach the wood to the metal frame using the 1-inch carriage bolts, flat washer, and nut. Make sure the carriage bolt head is on the outside of the frame and the washer and nut are on the inside of the box. Repeat on the other end. Tighten all of the nuts and bolts using the ⁷⁄₁₆-inch-long ratcheting socket wrench. Do not over-tighten or you may split the cedar.

Place the long cedar boards with predrilled holes and rounded edge on the long sides of the frame, rounded side up, making sure the countersunk

holes face inside the box and the rounded edge is right-side up facing the inside of the box. Match up the predrilled holes on the boards and legs, and attach the wood to the metal frame using the 1-inch carriage bolts, flat washer, and nut. Make sure the carriage bolt head is on the outside of the frame and the washer and nut are on the inside of the box. Repeat on the other side. Tighten all of the nuts and bolts using the ⁷⁄₁₆-inch-long ratcheting socket wrench. Do not over-tighten or you may split the cedar.

Repeat these steps for the short cedar boards.

Place the slats inside the box, leaving a small gap between the boards for drainage.

NOTE:

Freedom Growing recommends applying a finish or paint to the outside of the cedar before you assemble the box.

continued

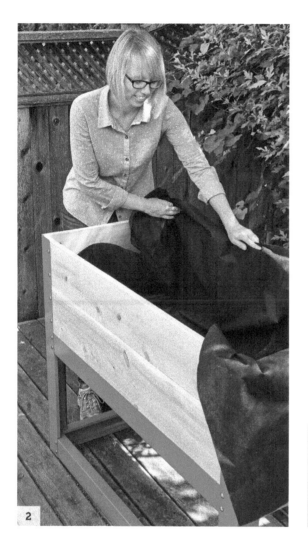

2. Line your raised bed.

Use the landscape fabric provided with the kit to line the box. Cedar will turn a grayish-silver color over time, so Freedom Growing recommends sealing or clear-coating the outside only of the cedar with a nontoxic clear sealer such as beeswax, linseed oil, or tung oil. These are available at most hardware stores. Sealing the wood will help extend the life of the cedar.

You can also turn your planter box into a mini greenhouse or cold frame by adding a cover.

Freedom Growing recommends that kit owners check the integrity of the wood every year before planting to make sure the cedar doesn't need replacing and that the nuts and bolts are still tight.

NOTE:

Depending on the soil type you use, a filled garden box can weigh as much as 200 pounds.

Plant It!

When planting from seed, keep an eye on how crowded your seedlings are once they start to poke up through the soil. As painful as it may be to throw away a baby plant, root vegetables need space around them to grow under the soil. So if the young plants are too close together, use your fingers or tweezers to gently pull the extraneous sprouts out of the soil and toss them in the compost. Beet sprouts are quite tasty, so those can just be rinsed and tossed in a salad.

This is what was planted in the washbasin pictured here:

- Early Wonder Tall Top beets
- Romeo baby carrots
- White Icicle radish
- Red-Cored Chantenay carrot
- Rainbow Swiss chard
- Leaf lettuce

Lettuce and chard will last a bit longer because it can be trimmed and used as needed, and then new growth keeps providing fresh leaves.

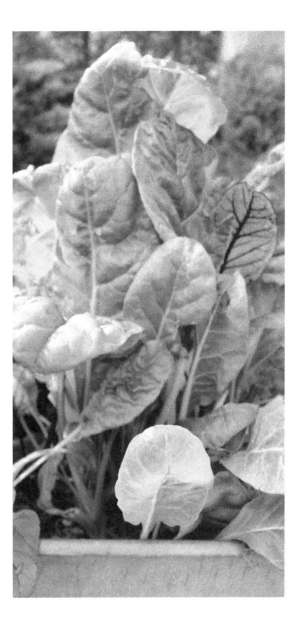

Cool-weather crops, such as beets, parsnips, and radishes, can be sown in early spring before the soil has completely warmed up. They can also be sown in late summer as a fall crop. That means you can enjoy fresh veggies sooner—and later—in the season.
Tara Nolan

Galvanized Steel and Wood Container

Designed by Scott McKinnon
Photography by *Donna Griffith*
Illustration by Len Churchill
Corrugated steel sheets courtesy of Conquest Steel;
shot on location at the Toronto Botanical Garden

There's something very modern-looking about galvanized steel paired with wood, especially once the wood is stained. For this project, corrugated steel sheets have been inlaid into a wooden frame, but they could just as easily be incorporated into a raised bed. This planter is the perfect size to tuck into a sunny corner of a patio or balcony. Wheels make it easy to move the container around with the sun—or into storage for the winter.

Tools

- Miter saw
- Power drill or impact driver
- Screwdriver (optional)
- Eye and ear protection
- Work gloves

Materials

- (3) 1 × 12" × 8' knotty pine boards (thickness is about 1")
- (2) 14 × 22" galvanized corrugated steel panels
- (4) 16 × 22" galvanized corrugated steel panels
- Exterior brass or anodized construction screws (¾", 1½")
- (4) 2" locking casters
- Scraps to create the removable slats along the bottom

Cut list

PART	DIMENSION	PCS
Frame, side pieces	1½ × 9¼ × 45"	2
Front and back panels	¾ × 2½ × 24"	6
Front and back panels	¾ × 2½ × 13¼"	8
Front and back panels	¾ × 2½ × 34"	4
Front and back panels	¾ × 2½ × 19"	6
End pieces	¾ × 2½ × 16"	4
End pieces	¾ × 2½ × 19"	4
End pieces	¾ × 1½ × 24"	4
End pieces	¾ × 2½ × 11"	4
Cleats	¾ × ¾ × 31½"	2

Bottom slats (measure from scrap)

front/back
corrugated galvanized
steel panels

front
inner stiles

front
top rails

side
outer top rail

side
inner top rail

front
outer
top rail

front
inner stile

bottom panel

cleat

side
inner stiles

side
corrugated galvanized
steel panel

side
outer stiles

front
outer stiles

front
outer bottom rail

front
bottom rails

caster

side
outer bottom rail

side
outer
bottom rail

TOP VIEW

2½"   2½"

34"

24"

16"

19"

OUTER FRONT VIEW

OUTER SIDE VIEW

34"

1½"   1½"

13¼"   13¼"

11"

24"

INNER FRONT VIEW

INNER SIDE VIEW

continued

To Make the Galvanized Steel and Wood Container

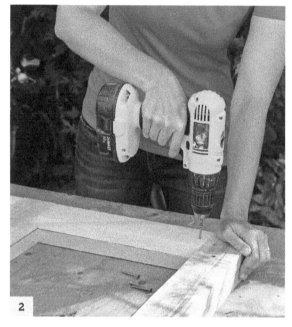

1. Start the front and back panels.

To create the front panel, lay out the three 2½ × 24-inch pieces in a row, and place the four 2½ × 13¼-inch pieces horizontally between them. Be sure that all edges and corners are lined up. These pieces will be facing the inside of the planter.

2. Add reinforcements and build the side pieces.

On top of this layout, place the 2½ × 34-inch pieces horizontally along the top and bottom and then three 2½ × 19-inch pieces on the ends and in the middle. Attach with screws. This is the outside-facing front and back of the planter. Repeat these steps to make the back panel.

To make the end pieces, lay the 16-inch pieces horizontally with two 19-inch pieces between them for the vertical pieces. On top of this frame, lay the 1½ × 24-inch pieces vertically along the inside edge of the frame, leaving an equal amount of space on either side. This is to accommodate the front and back panels during assembly. Place the 11-inch pieces horizontally between them across the top and bottom. Attach with screws.

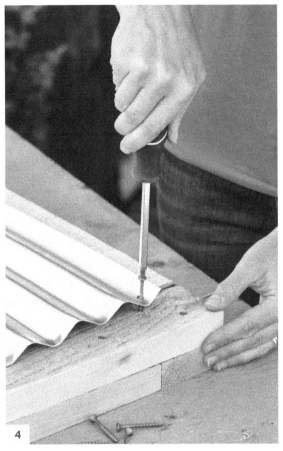

3. Position the metal sheets.

Lay the 16-inch pieces of corrugated metal on top of the openings on the inside of the front and back panels.

4. Attach the metal.

Predrill holes using a ⅛ or ³⁄₁₆-inch high-speed steel (HSS) bit. Fasten the metal to the wood using ¾-inch screws. Repeat for the side panels using the 14-inch pieces of metal.

continued

5. Put the box together.

On your work surface, place a front panel perpendicular to the corner of a side panel and drill the two pieces together using 1½-inch screws. Repeat for all sides. Note that the narrower vertical strips on the inside of the end panels will allow the corners to come together more closely.

Add a shelf for the false bottom.

Cut two pieces of wood for the cleats that are ¾ × ¾ × 31½ inches. Turn the box upside down and attach the cleats with 1½-inch screws flush with the bottom of the long sides. Then nail them flush with the inside of the bottom of the panels. Use three planks measured and cut from the remaining knotty pine to rest on top of them. It's okay if there are small gaps between the slats because this is an essential part of allowing water to drain from the planter.

6

6. Put the box on wheels.

Turn the project over and attach the casters with the screws that came with your casters (or ones purchased to fit them).

(See False-Bottom Fakery, page 118, to discover how you can avoid filling this entire planter with soil.)

The outside of the container was finished with a solid waterborne exterior stain. Admittedly, it might be easier to paint your pieces before putting the project together!

This planter is essentially bottomless until you install cleats onto which you can rest three removable slats cut from the remaining lumber. This allows water to drain out the bottom. The slats also can be easily replaced if they eventually succumb to rot, without having to take the entire planter apart. Furthermore, if the plan is for the planter to sit right on the ground, you actually don't have to add in a bottom at all.

This planter is rather heavy once it's been built, so the addition of rolling and locking casters means it can easily be rolled into a shed or garage, or onto a dolly, when you're placing it into storage for the winter.

Upcycled Suitcase Planter with Gas Pipe Legs

Designed by Scott McKinnon
Photography by *Donna Griffith*
Illustration by Len Churchill

Antique markets and yard sales can be a treasure trove of innovative raised bed ideas. This project gave new purpose to an old wooden suitcase by transforming it into a small raised bed. Legs made from pieces of threaded gas pipe give it a modern touch. This little garden would make a perfect addition to a small patio or balcony. It's kind of like a window box without the window needing to be there.

Any wooden box will do—you can also keep an eye out for wooden wine or apple crates. And if you don't happen to have an old suitcase or box of some type, you could easily whip one together.

The suitcase planter pictured here has been filled with both edibles and ornamentals, so it's not only pretty, it's practical—and delicious!

Tools

- Screwdriver, power drill or impact driver
- Tape measure
- Old rag to handle gas pipe parts
- Eye protection
- Work gloves

NOTE:

You may choose to use a bigger or smaller box. With different dimensions, you may choose to use different pipe lengths and diameters.

Materials

FOR THE TOP:

- Shallow wooden box (we used an old suitcase about 24¼ × 17¾ × 5⅝")

FOR THE LEGS:

- ½" threaded black gas pipe (this is the pipe that's generally used to transport natural or propane gas from the street to a house) was used for this project. You could use a different width for a chunkier look, depending on the aesthetic you want.

- (4) floor/wall flanges

- (4) end caps (for the feet)

- 6½" tee fittings

- 1½" union (middle)

- (4) 24" pieces pipe threaded on each end

- (6) 6" pieces threaded pipe (also called pipe nipples)

- (4) 3½" pieces threaded pipe (also called pipe nipples)

- (16) screws (length depends on the thickness of the wood; we used #10 × ½" but could use longer if you have thicker wood)

floor/wall flange

existing or shop-made box with drain holes

24" pipe threaded on each end

3½" pipe threaded on each end

6" pipe threaded on each end

end cap (foot)

1½" union

½" tee fitting

continued

How to Make a Upcycled Suitcase Planter with Gas Pipe Legs

1. Prep the box.

Prepare the box that will rest on top of the gas pipe legs. Here, the top of the suitcase was removed simply by unscrewing part of the hinge. The hinges were left on the actual box as decoration.

2. Drill drainage holes.

Add holes to the bottom of your box. Lay it aside for now.

3. Assemble all pipe pieces.

Have a rag close at hand as you put the gas pipe parts together; they can be quite greasy.

Screw one flange into one end of each 24-inch pipe. On the other end, add a tee fitting.

To continue the leg, add one 6-inch pipe to the opposite end of the tee. To the end of that, screw on the end cap. To the perpendicular end of the tee, add a 3½-inch threaded pipe. Repeat for the three other legs.

Use a tee to connect each set of end legs. Your project should now be in two pieces. Attach the two sets of end legs by screwing the 6-inch pieces of pipe to the middle tees of the two leg sets so they'll be parallel to the ground. Attach them with one union. It will take a bit of maneuvering to twist everything so it's just so and the feet rest on the ground evenly.

4. **Determine the perfect leg placement on the box.**

Set the whole leg construction with the flanges touching the box, and measure where they will go so you can screw them in place.

5. **Assemble the top and bottom.**

Attach the flanges to the box with screws. When you turn it back over, the box can be leveled by twisting various sections of pipe as needed to make it longer or shorter.

Line the box with landscape fabric; fill with soil to prepare it for planting.

Finishing the legs

When left outdoors, the gas pipe legs will develop a natural rust-colored patina. Be careful where you place the new raised bed, however, because you don't want the rust to leach onto the surface. To protect the gas pipe legs from rusting, apply a couple of coats of tung oil (a food-grade oil) with a brush or a rag, wiping it off between coats. You could also use a rustproof spray paint—either a clear coat or a vibrant color.

A Quick Vertical Gardening Pallet Project

Pallets have really proven their versatility in the last few years, becoming one of the most popular items that creative DIYers refurbish into a variety of household pieces. Some construction sites and even stores that get big shipments give them away for free, while others have tried to cash in on the humble pallet's popularity by charging for them. Pallets have been reimagined into everything from coffee tables and outdoor sofas to vertical gardens, which can technically be categorized as a type of raised bed, like the one shown here. Even some of the wood strips that you'll see on our Raised Bed with Upcycled Wood Design (page 46) came from pallets that had been taken apart.

Built to withstand extreme weight, pallets are generally made from hardwoods. When sourcing pallets for a project, be mindful of where you get them—you want to make sure they haven't been subjected to any toxic chemicals. Look for the letters HT, which stands for heat-treated (instead of chemical-treated). But avoid the letters MB because that means the pallet has been fumigated with methyl bromide. Avoid pallets with warped wood or cracked edges, or that look as though they've been painted or stained. You don't want anything leaching into your garden, especially if you're growing food. If you're unsure, stick to planting ornamentals in your vertical garden.

Not only can pallets be used for practical purposes, they can be great ornamental features in a garden, as well. *Tara Nolan*

Prepare your pallet by cleaning it and reattaching any loose boards. Sand all the rough sides and edges on the outward-facing side with 80-grit sandpaper attached to an orbital sander.

If your pallet has open spaces along what will be the back side, you can use a staple gun and stainless-steel staples to attach a piece of hardware cloth to it so that soil cannot escape.

If the pallet is really open along the front-facing side, create pockets with the landscape fabric, or you can use 2 × 2s to create shelves that are attached to the lower edge of each slat. The one area you want to ensure is covered is the bottom.

To plant your pallet, lay it out flat on the ground and fill with soil. Add your plants, being sure to place them close together. Water everything thoroughly. Then leave the pallet on its side for a few days to allow the roots to grow; this will help the soil stay in place when you pick it up and lean it where it's going to stay.

Four edibles that grow well in a pallet garden

Lettuces work well in a pallet for the same reason that they work well in a lettuce table: they have shallow root systems. Choose a mix of leafy greens for a flavorful salad mix.

A medley of herbs, from thyme and oregano to chives and parsley, will do well planted within the spaces of a pallet.

Nasturtiums also make great pallet plants because they will cascade over the sides as the season progresses. Both the blooms and leaves are edible!

Strawberry plants produce runners that will also spill over the sides of a pallet.

Tips for Adding Raised Beds to a Balcony or Rooftop Patio

Having a small space does not put you at a disadvantage. You can still have a garden that yields a decent harvest yet goes beyond the basics of a couple of herbs and a tomato plant. You just need to get creative with your space.

Will there be challenges? Yes. However, there are some advantages too. For example, you won't attract the same level of pests that can attack plants in a backyard garden—at least nothing of the four-legged variety. You won't be totally immune to insect pests, but there shouldn't be as many to contend with. Unfortunately your garden will not benefit from the good guys, like worms. And, because you are creating a self-contained eco-system, you will need to replenish your soil more often. New soil should be used every year.

If your balcony or rooftop patio gets six to eight hours of sunshine a day, you're in luck because you can tick "proper growing conditions" off your list of planting requirements. All you need is a raised bed—albeit one that is more compact—that fits into your small space.

Balconies are built to withstand extra weight from people, snow load, and so on, but to minimize putting added stress on a balcony, opt

© *Les Urbainculteurs / Smart Pots*

for lightweight materials for your raised bed, and choose soil mixes that are fluffy. Compressed mixes exist specifically for these types of gardens. If you're building from a kit, look for a light, modular one that can easily be built on-site.

There are, however, a few elements that will differ when you're gardening several floors up rather than on terra firma. First and foremost, you can't toss everything into a wheelbarrow or make several trips back and forth to the backyard from the car. You're likely dealing with an elevator—or maybe even stairs. Consider what you have to lug up and down, what you may have to store over the winter, as well as the fact that you'll be carrying all your materials, plants, and soil through your apartment or condo.

Here are a few more things to take into consideration when you're planting in the sky.

Read your building's rules

Before you invest time and money into a garden, carefully read the legal and safety requirements for your building. You need to consider the weight of your raised beds once they're full of soil as well as drainage issues. Avoid heavy materials like concrete.

Keep in mind that terraces may be considered a common element, meaning that the building owns the outdoor space and the owner has the exclusive usage rights to it. Your setup, whatever it may be, should have zero impact on the building.

Most regulations emphasize that you should not install a planter that someone could technically step up on, putting them in danger if it's close to a balcony railing. Consult with your building management if you're not sure what's permitted and what is not.

Check zoning laws

Depending on how big your balcony garden will be, you may want to check not only your building regulations but also zoning laws, or even an architect, to assess the impact of the weight of your garden.

Devise a watering plan

Keep in mind that during the steamy summer months, gardens can dry out quickly in the hot sun, so some containers may need to be watered twice a day.

© Les Urbainculteurs / Smart Pots

Most balconies don't have the luxury of access to an outdoor tap so you may want to consider a watering setup that has a built-in reservoir.

On a roof, a small holding tank could be used to store rainwater that is then distributed to the plants via a dripline irrigation system.

Drainage is important, but you want to make sure any overflow isn't dripping onto a neighbor's space. You can use small trays with planters that don't have a built-in reservoir to hold water.

Fabric pots are also an option because they drain well and provide good aeration around the roots.

Master the false bottom

Depending on the size of the raised bed you place on your balcony or rooftop, keep in mind that you don't need to fill the entire thing with soil. Packing peanuts, for example, make good space fillers. They're light and readily available, and water drains through them easily.

Another way to take up space in your planter is to line the sides with Styrofoam or ¼-inch insulation sheets. Just be sure to line the sides with landscape fabric first.

And there's a bonus to lining the sides of your balcony-sized raised bed: if you happen to leave it outdoors over the winter and the soil freezes solid, it won't split open the sides.

(See False-Bottom Fakery, page 118, for more tips.)

Chapter 4

Raised Beds with Purpose

There's no denying that all raised beds are built with a purpose in mind. But the ones in this chapter go a step further from the typical raised bed in their function and utility. While raised beds are versatile enough that you can pretty much grow anything in them, the beds in this chapter tend to have more of a singular purpose.

For those who want to test their green thumb growing spuds, a stackable potato bin makes it especially easy for first-timers.

Season extenders figure into this purpose-driven chapter with a cleverly constructed greenhouse that fits right over a raised bed and a cold frame made from an upcycled window that dispels the notion that there is only one growing season. They can both be used to harden off seedlings, store plants that need to go dormant, and extend the season, allowing fresh greens and root veggies to be picked during the winter months.

Rolling casters, as exemplified on a Versailles-inspired raised bed, are a boon to gardeners, allowing them to freely move plants into sunlight, storage, or wherever it is they need to go.

There are a few other inspiring ideas with unique purposes to be discovered. Hopefully it sparks your imagination to add some raised beds that will take your garden to the next level.

Potato-Growing Box

Designed and written by Chris Peterson
Photography by Tracy Walsh
Illustration by Bill Kersey

Digging up potatoes has to be one of the most satisfying parts of the harvest. Perhaps it's because you really don't know what's happening underneath the soil until it's time to dig up your potatoes, whereas with edibles that fruit on branches, you can ascertain right away the likelihood of growing a successful crop.

This special raised bed construction also makes it easier to harvest your spuds, as you simply lift off the layers one at a time (be sure to have something on hand to catch the soil) to reveal the tasty tubers.

Tools

- Table saw or circular saw
- Drill
- Mallet
- Chisel
- Carpenter's square
- Tape measure
- Eye and ear protection
- Work gloves

Materials

- (5) 2" × 6" × 8'
- (1) 2 × 2 × 8'
- 2½" deck screws

Cut list

PART	DIMENSION	PCS
Box sides	1½ × 5½ × 29½"	16
Box cleats	1½ × 1½ × 5"	16

box sides

cleats

29½"

5½"

1⁹⁄₁₆"

2"

2¾"

5"

continued

How to Make a Potato-Growing Box

1. Cut the box sides.

Carefully cut the sides for the box. All the pieces need to be exactly the same dimensions and the ends perfectly square. Lay out the half-lap notches on two of the boards as shown, making each 1⁹⁄₁₆ inches wide. Screw a straight board to the sliding miter gauge to keep the sides straight as you push them through. The depth of each notch is exactly half of the board's width, so measure the boards and adjust the depth as needed. Align and clamp the boards to the miter gauge. Make the first cut at 2 inches from the end, and then slide the boards over 1⁹⁄₁₆ inches and make the second cut. (You can also use a circular saw or a jigsaw to make these cuts.)

2. Hone your half-lap notches.

Break off the waste material and clean up the bottom of the notch with a sharp chisel. Check the fit. If everything looks good, cut the rest of the boards on the table saw. If you're using a circular saw, trace the notches onto the remaining boards with a sharp pencil and then cut out all of the remaining notches.

> **NOTE:**
>
> Only the bottom layer of boards has to be the exact same depth. If it's a little deep, you can drive a screw in at the base and turn it in or out to make the top edges level.

3

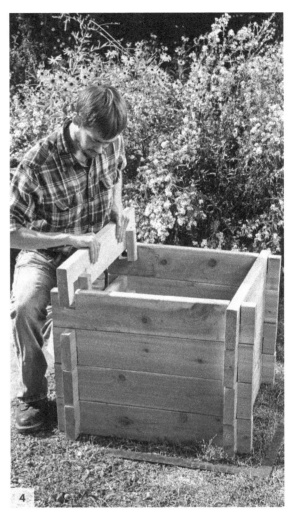

4

3. Prepare and install the cleats.

Use a square to mark positioning lines for the cleats on each board, marking the lines just to the inside of each notch. These represent the outside faces of the 2 × 2-inch cleats. Mark a vertical line 3 inches above the base of each notch; this represents the top end of each cleat. Install the cleats by drilling countersunk pilot holes, and fastening the cleats to the boards with pairs of 2½-inch deck screws.

> **NOTE:**
>
> For the bottom course of the box, you can omit the cleats, if desired, or you can make longer cleats with pointed ends to help anchor the box to the ground.

4. Take a test run.

Test-fit the parts by assembling the entire box. Use a carpenter's square or measure diagonally between opposing corners of the box frame to make sure the frame is square. Plant your seed potatoes about four to eight inches deep, and cover with soil or mulch. As the plants spring out of the ground, add more soil and additional pieces until the box is complete.

Cold Frame Using an Old Window

Designed by Deon Haupt and Tara Nolan
Photography by *Donna Griffith*
Illustration by Len Churchill

Have you ever picked a fresh salad during the winter solstice? Many gardeners might think that the growing season ends in autumn once the last fruits of the harvest have been picked. However, a season extender will keep green thumbs stocked with root vegetables and greens all winter long. Enter the mighty cold frame. This simple contraption has a clear glass or plastic top that harnesses the sun's winter rays, keeps plants warm enough to grow, and prevents them from freezing into ice cubes. In fact, depending on the day, it just might get too hot in there. You may need to crack the top open and let some fresh, frosty air in! An indoor/outdoor thermometer will help you keep tabs on the temperature. Also, keep in mind that after a storm, you need to make sure to clear away the snow from the lid. The result is fresh, unexpected produce throughout the winter.

Tools

- Miter saw
- Circular saw or jigsaw
- Japanese dozuki saw
- Orbital sander or sandpaper
- Power drill or impact driver
- Straight edge and pencil
- Clamps (optional)
- Tape measure
- Eye and ear protection
- Work gloves

Materials

- (4) 2" × 6" × 8' cedar boards
- (2) hinges
- 2¾" screws

Cut list

PART	DIMENSION	PCS
Front and back pieces	1½ × 5½ × 32¼"	5
Side pieces	1½ × 5½ × 30"	4
Angled side pieces (see instructions)	1½ × 5½ × 30"	2
Corner braces (cut from scrap)	2½ × 6 × 16½"	2
Corner braces (cut from scrap)	2½ × 6 × 11"	2

NOTE:

This project was made to accommodate an old window that's 32¼" long × 30" wide.

hinge spacers

existing framed window

angled
side panel

corner braces

front panels

side panels

30"

SIDE VIEW

continued

How to Make a Cold Frame Using an Old Window

1. Build the frame.

Lay out the 32¼-inch front and back pieces so that they cover the sides of the 30-inch side pieces to form a box. Screw in place to make the bottom of the frame. Repeat this step to create the second layer. For the third layer, there is a back piece but no front piece because of the angled slope you want to create once the window is attached. This means the side pieces need to be cut at an angle. They also need to be longer to accommodate the slope. Leave about 10 inches on the end in order to either screw or clamp the work piece down to your bench for when you make the cut. Screw the side piece to the back piece temporarily, and place on top of the box. Take a straight edge and place it from the edge of the top corner to the front of the box diagonally across the board and draw a line.

Remove the temporary screws and attach the extra 10-inch length to your work table with clamps or screws. Use a circular saw or jigsaw to slowly cut

it out as you're going across the grain. One cut gives you both angled side pieces. Trim the extra 10 inches off the one piece to length.

2. Sand the side pieces.

Use an orbital sander or sandpaper to smooth the rough edges of the angled side pieces.

3. Attach the angled side pieces.

Place the two angled side pieces inside the edges of the third back piece and fasten in place from the back. There is no front piece for the third level of this assembly because of the angle of the final project.

Add an extra screw on each side toward the front to secure the side pieces in place because they will not attach to the corner braces.

4. Install the corner braces.

From one of the remaining cedar boards, cut two pieces that are 2½ × 16½ inches and two pieces that are 2½ × 11 inches. The long pieces are the braces for the back corners. Cut the ends of these on a slight angle to accommodate the gentle slope of the tops of the angled side pieces, or you can cut a bit shorter and install them below the angle. The window should close without leaving a gap further down. From the inside, screw these four braces to the outside frame to secure it in place.

6. Attach the hinges.

The preexisting metal piece along the back of the old window would have prevented the screws for the hinges from going in, so two scrap pieces of wood were trimmed and used to create a new "back" to which the hinges could be attached. This also pushed the window forward a bit to make up for the extra centimeters that were added from the diagonal. Once these scraps are screwed in place, attach the two hinges to the window frame and the frame of the box.

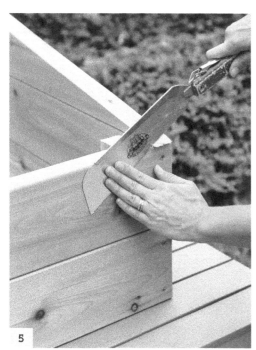

5. Trim the front.

If there is a bit of wood from the two angled pieces overlapping the front, use a dozuki handsaw or the orbital sander to gently trim it away.

Greenhouse Cover for Raised Bed

Designed and written by Jamie Gilgen
Photography by *Donna Griffith*
Illustration by Len Churchill

Just as a cold frame helps to prolong the growing season—or get a head start on it—a greenhouse also adds more flexibility to your planting options. Jamie Gilgen, a professional cyclist—and a skilled woodworker and green thumb—created this version of a greenhouse to fit over one of the raised beds she built. Gilgen is often away competing in cycling competitions, so she needed something that would allow her to protect a bountiful harvest despite not being in the garden every day to be able to vent her greenhouse.

A clever contraption called an automatic opener features a gas-charged cylinder that expands as the temperature inside the greenhouse climbs, prompting the arm that's attached to immediately and automatically prop open the side of the greenhouse. Venting is important when temperatures fluctuate so that you don't inadvertently cook the vegetables that are growing within.

In the summer, the design allows Gilgen to simply remove the side flaps of the greenhouse altogether so that the plants can breathe and thrive in their spot in the garden without having to move them.

Gilgen has generously shared her plans here to recreate this greenhouse that fits over a raised bed. You can modify the measurements to make it fit yours.

This plan is for a greenhouse that measures 4 × 5 feet × 18 inches at the base of the roof. The total height is 42 inches.

Tools

- A saw that can make cuts at a specific depth, such as a miter saw, table saw or circular saw
- Drill
- Drill bits
- Screwdriver
- Staple gun
- Eye and ear protection
- Work gloves

Materials

- Wood glue
- (14) 2 × 2" × 8'
- 3½" wood screws
- 1½" wood screws
- (2) Long wood screws with bolt ends
- Vapor barrier (6mil plastic film)
- (4) Hinges
- Stainless-steel staples

Bonus Options

- Heat-activated opener from Lee Valley
- Outdoor paint

roof flap rail

roof truss

roof flap stile

roof rails

side rails

side stile

front rails

front stile

1¾"

⅞" x 1¾" half lap joint

CORNER – TOP VIEW

45°

SIDE VIEW

How to Make a Greenhouse Cover for Raised Bed

1. Create the frame.

To create a rectangular frame that will act as the base of the greenhouse, you will need the following:

Cut two pieces of 2 × 2s to 5 feet long each, and cut two pieces of 2 × 2s 18 inches long each.

Lap joints are used in this project to join the lengths of wood together, which will result in a more rigid structure. Lap joints are the secret to being able to use 2 × 2s to build this structure and still have it be very sturdy. You could use butt joints, but the structure wouldn't be nearly as strong.

How to make a lap joint To make lap joints, at the end of each of the four lengths that have just been cut, make a cut that is halfway through the wood and the same width as your lumber. If it's a 2 × 2, this is normally around 1¾ inches. If you have a tablesaw with a dado blade, this will be a very simple exercise; but if you don't, that's okay, it will just be a bit more manual. Once you have one cut that matches up with the width, create many more until you reach the end of the length. Then, use a chisel to remove the slivers of wood that are remaining. You will be doing this procedure a total of eight times, once for each end of wood.

Once you've completed the cuts, dry-assemble your pieces and make sure all the joints line up properly. Make any adjustments necessary. Drill pilot holes through each joint; these will be used to screw the joints together for even more strength.

After all of your pieces have been drilled, spread some glue on each surface of the joints. Make sure everything is aligned, and use a 1½-inch screw to join them together.

Once all of this is done, you will have completed one side of the greenhouse. Repeat this procedure and you will have completed both sides of the greenhouse.

You're now half done with the rectangular frame of the greenhouse. Repeat all of the above steps, but cut lengths from 2 × 2 stock using the following equation: 4' - (2" × 1¾") = 44.5". This is the same equation used for the roof truss.

2. Create the roof.

The roof is built at a 45-degree angle so that it sheds snow well. This is especially important if you'll be using this structure as a cold frame. The roof is very simple: It consists of two lengths of 2 × 2 cut at 45-degree angles on each end.

Cuts for the roof Cut four lengths of wood. They should be cut to 35½ inches long. Use a miter saw to cut each end at a 45-degree angle, so that when the two pieces are assembled, they butt together making a 90-degree angle and each end lays flat and true against the frame.

For the main roof truss, use another 2 × 2, and cut it to 5 feet minus 2 × the actual width of your lumber. For example, truss length = (5' × 12") - 2 × 1.75" = 56½".

Securing the joints Drill pilot holes slightly offset so that you can screw each end of the roof at the apex together. Also drill two pilot holes on each end that will attach to the frame. Glue up the pieces, and screw them together. There are no fancy joints in this part of the structure.

For the main roof truss, drill through the apex of the two roof beams into the end of the main truss. This should be a deep hole and larger because you'll be using a very large bolt to secure it.

3. Create the roof flaps

You'll be creating two roof flaps so that you can access the greenhouse from both sides. If you only want one flap, that's fine although I recommend two because this greenhouse is 4 feet wide and that's a long way to reach with only one flap.

For each flap, cut two pieces of 2 × 2 to 5 feet long and two pieces of 2 × 2 to about 34 inches long. Use your freshly honed lap joint skills to join the top two joints of each flap; for the bottom one, there is a special step. If you do not have a tablesaw that can cut at 45-degree angles, see below. Cut one of the 5-foot lengths at a 45-degree angle all the way across. This is a tricky cut, so if you have someone to help you, it's much safer. Once this is done, you should be able to just drill a pilot hole through the ends of the roof flap and butt joint it together.

I don't have a tablesaw If you don't have a tablesaw, you can just join the flaps like you did the other four sides of the greenhouse. The flap just won't sit perfectly flat at the interface between the rectangular structure and the flap.

4. Assemble all your parts.

You now have two long rectangles and two short rectangles with triangles on top. If you don't want to be able to disassemble the greenhouse, just screw it all together. If you do, drill large holes and bolt it together. Once you have your rectangular base assembled, bolt in the main roof truss using the two large pilot holes made earlier. Now attach the flaps using the hinges.

5. Wrap your greenhouse.

You now have a sizable structure, but it's not a greenhouse yet. Cut pieces of a 6mil vapor barrier larger than each of the main areas of the frame. Staple them in place and cut off any excess. Use stainless-steel staples, if you can find them. It keeps your greenhouse looking pristine and rust-free. The vapor barrier expands and shrinks a lot with temperature, so wrap it at around 50°F to avoid ripping and flapping.

Option: Add an automatic opener.

If you don't want to have to worry about cooking your precious plants, you can install an automatic opener. Cut two pieces of wood, and screw them into the frame. If you used untreated wood, be sure to add some type of finish to the outside to protect it.

Versailles-Inspired Planter

Designed by Scott McKinnon
Photography by Donna Griffith
Illustration by Len Churchill

The inspiration behind the design of this versatile planter has royal roots. André Le Nôtre, King Louis XIV's gardener, is said to have designed the first "Versailles planter" in 1670 for the orange trees that were imported to Versailles, France. These tropical specimens that provided fruit to the court would not have survived the winter weather in this region of France. The solution was to plant them in portable containers that could be moved from the formal gardens into a greenhouse called an "orangerie" during the coldest months of the year.

Tools

- Miter saw
- Hammer or pneumatic nailer
- Sandpaper or rounding plane
- Bevel square or carpenter's square and a pencil
- Power drill or impact driver
- Eye and ear protection
- Work gloves

Materials

- (4) 2½" casters
- (1) ¾" 4' × 8' sheet exterior plywood
- (1 box) 1½" exterior screws
- (12) ½" × 1¾" × 10' cedar strips
- (1 box) Finishing nails

Cut list

PART	DIMENSION	PCS
Box side	18 × 18"	2
Box side	16½ × 18"	2
Box bottom	16½ × 16½"	1
Cedar strips	18"	48
Top edge	Measure to fit	4
"X" pattern	Measure to fit	8

top strips

wide side panel

narrow side panel

narrow side panel

wide side panel

side corner strips

side corner strip

caster

vertical cedar strips

horizontal strip

long diagonal strip

short diagonal strip

18"

SIDE VIEW

18"

16"

TOP VIEW

continued

How to Make a Versailles-Inspired Planter

1. Cut the box pieces.

Cut two pieces of plywood 18 × 18 inches (for side pieces) and two pieces of plywood 16½ × 18 inches (for the other side pieces). Cut one piece of plywood 16½ × 16½ inches (for the bottom). Assemble the plywood box with the smaller sides inside the larger ones, and the bottom panel enclosed on all sides. Attach with screws.

2. Finish all the edges.

With a rounding plane or sandpaper, round the long edges of all the cedar strips. This gives them a nice finished edge.

3. Create the cedar strips.

Cut 48 pieces of cedar strip to 18 inches each. Lay 10 pieces out per side, nailing them on vertically with finishing nails.

4. Attach the side corners.

To make a side corner, place two strips perpendicular to each other so that each piece meets evenly at the corner of the box. They'll form an L shape. Nail the strips tight. Repeat for all the other corners.

Measure for the horizontal strips that run between the corner pieces along the top and the bottom.

Note: Lapping the corners as was done in the previous step could alter the measurements for these pieces a little. Be sure to measure them before cutting. Attach these eight strips (top and bottom on all four sides) by nailing in place.

5. Make the top of the box.

To make the top edge of the planter, start by taking a longer piece of cedar and measuring the inside lengths of the planter. This is the measurement you want so you can cut two opposing 45-degree angles on either end so all the pieces meet evenly in the corners. Continue to measure and cut all the way around. Nail everything in place.

6. Measure and cut to form the X.

Lay a piece from corner to corner, and line it up how you want in the corners. Mark with a pencil the angled cut you'll need to make it fit in. It should be 45 degrees or very close depending on how you've laid out the box. For the cross piece, mark out where it's going to need to be cut out in the center so that the two pieces fit snugly around the other half of the X. Repeat for all sides.

continued

7

7. Add casters.

Turn the planter over, and place the casters at the edges of the plywood.

Predrill the holes for the casters' screws using a ¼-inch wood bit. Attach the casters with the screws and add a nut and bolt from the inside to secure in place. Add casters.

Turn the planter over, and place the casters at the edges of the plywood.

Predrill the holes for the casters' screws using a ¼-inch wood bit. Attach the casters with the screws and add a nut and bolt from the inside to secure in place.

What does a rounding plane do?

To give this planter a more refined look, a mini handheld edge-rounding plane created slightly curved and smooth edges in the wood. The one used for this project could be used on the push stroke, creating the desired effect in one or two passes.

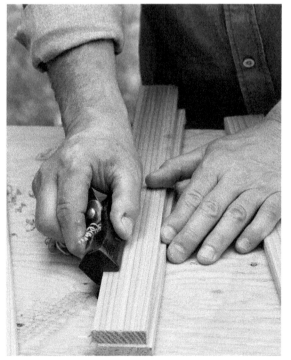

Other Uses for Cold Frames

Besides being used to grow fresh crops during the cold, winter months, a cold frame can also come in handy for other functions—if it's empty, of course. Here are a few:

HARDEN OFF SEEDLINGS. When it's time to bring the wee little plants that you've grown indoors from seed out into the garden, you need to allow them to adapt to the elements. You can't just set them out in the sun because the delicate baby plants are not used to the hot rays or wind. Usually this means bringing plants outside to a protected spot for a few hours at a time, and then bringing them in at night over the course of a few days. A cold frame provides a perfect protected spot for plants to get used to being outdoors.

STORE NURSERY PLANTS. It's tempting to purchase plants at the nursery before the ground is ready for them. You can temporarily store impulse purchases in your cold frame—being sure to vent it if it gets too hot—until you're ready to put them in the garden.

GROW PERENNIAL SEEDS AND PROPAGATE CUTTINGS. Protect new plants that you've grown from seed or propagated from woody cuttings in your cold frame over the winter. Give them a little extra protection by covering them lightly with dry leaves or evergreen branches.

OVERWINTER PLANTS THAT GO DORMANT. Some plants simply shut down over the winter. Provided they're not too big, these can be placed inside a cold frame to comfortably hibernate until spring.

GET A HEAD START BY PLANTING HARDY ANNUALS. As you wait for the ground to thaw, your cold frame can become a mini greenhouse, allowing you to grow a variety of plants from seed.

Once you have a regular raised bed, you'll want to add the indispensable cold frame to your garden inventory. *Sean James*

Protected Strawberry Planter

Designed and written by Chris Peterson
Photography by Tracy Walsh
Illustration by Bill Kersey

Strawberries are one of those first fruits of spring and summer that you'll find at the farmers' market. And there's something about heading to a local pick-your-own farm that really jump-starts a harvest season full of fresh preserves, healthy salads, and produce-packed smoothies. It's likely that the abundance of these delectable fruits available during strawberry season is due to the fact that the plants are so easy for farmers to grow.

Did you know that you could set up your own pick-your-own farm right in your backyard? Just be warned: unfortunately, animals and birds enjoy these sweet treats too.

Enter this 69-inch-wide octagonal raised bed. Voracious spreaders such as mint and chamomile get a bad rap, but strawberries are also pretty good at spreading out. Not only does this ingenious

bed contain the plants, a handy lid lined with bird netting allows you to keep the fruit all to yourself—without having to share it with a neighborhood menagerie.

According to project designer Chris Peterson, building the planter frame can easily be done with a power miter saw. But you can also use a circular saw or a handsaw and a tall miter box. To increase or decrease the size of this raised bed, you can cut shorter or longer pieces. And, if you wish to change the shape of the planter, double the number of sides and divide that number into 360. (For example, a hexagon has six sides; therefore: 360 ÷ 12 = 30. Make each end cut at 30 degrees, and you'll have a perfect hexagon.)

Tools

- Miter saw
- Cordless drill and bits
- Speed square
- Eye and ear protection
- Work gloves

Materials

- Waterproof wood glue
- 3" deck screws
- Bird netting
- (4) 2 × 4" × 8' boards
- (24') screen molding

Cut list

PART	DIMENSION	PCS
Planter side	1½ × 3½ × 28½"	8
Cover support	¼ × ¾ × 72"	4

continued

How to Make a Protected Strawberry Planter

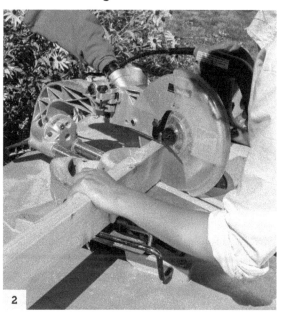

1.   Set up your miter saw.

Run some test cuts to make sure the angle setting is accurate. Cut two pieces of scrap 2 × 4 at 22½ degrees. Fit the pieces together end to end, and check the assembly with a straight edge; the pieces should be perfectly straight. (If you're using a circular saw, cut test pieces with the saw blade tilted at 22½ degrees.)

2.   Cut all sides to the same length.

Use a stop block setup to ensure that all pieces are precisely the same length. This speeds your work and ensures the joints will fit tightly. For this roughly 6-foot-wide planter, each piece is 28½ inches long, measuring between the long points of the two angled ends. To make the cuts, leave the miter saw set on one side and just flip the board over for each successive cut.

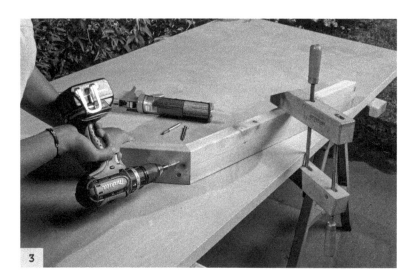

3.   Drill pilot holes.

Drill pilot holes through one frame piece and into its mating piece, starting the hole about ⅞ inch from the pointed end of the first piece. Angle the hole slightly toward the inside of the joint (what will be the inside of the assembled frame). This gives the screws a little bit of cross-grain penetration, helping them hold better than if they were perfectly parallel to the grain of the mating piece.

4. Assemble your octagonal shape.

Apply glue and fasten each joint with two screws. For extra strength, add a third screw driven from the opposite direction as the first two.

TIP

Work on a flat surface, such as a garage floor, to help keep the pieces flush at the top and bottom so the entire assembly will be flat.

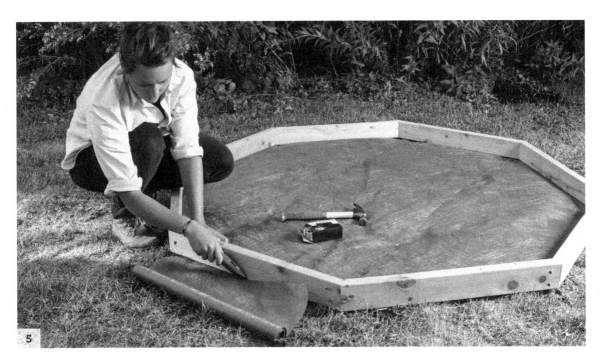

5. Prepare your planting site.

Dig out the grass and soil at least several inches deep and replace it with high-quality garden soil mix. Cover the soil with landscape fabric to keep unwanted grass or weeds from growing. Use nails or spikes to hold the fabric in place; then trim it flush with the octagon edges.

continued

6. Make the domed lid.

Create an arched dome with wooden screen molding (¼ × ¾ × 72-inch strips of wood). Predrill holes at each end for screws, using a drill bit bigger than the size of the screw. Mark the centers of each 2 × 4. Screw one end in, leaving the screw about ½ inch out of the wood. Move to the opposite side, arch the wood, and put a screw in on that side, tightening it just enough to hold the end down. Join the frame rails to the stiles with a metal corner at each stile.

7. Plant your strawberries.

Spread an inch or two of mulch over the landscape fabric, then plant the octagon with your strawberry plants. Cut slits in the fabric where each plant goes, and then work the plant down into the garden soil.

8. Add the protective netting.

Spread bird netting over the dome. Hold it in place by hooking it on two roundhead screws or small nails on each side. Trim the excess. To take the netting off, wrap one side around a piece of smooth wood or a 6-foot-long pole and just roll it up. When you want to cover the strawberries in the spring, just hook one side and roll it out again.

Chapter 5

Not Handy? No Problem!

If you don't consider yourself particularly handy, fear not. There are so many raised bed options, from upcycling items such as old drawers and fruit crates, to using newfangled containers like fabric pots and plastic bins, to assembling easy-to-follow kits.

Raid your (or someone else's) shed, attic, basement, or property for items that you can repurpose into a raised bed—old washtubs, dresser drawers, bathtubs, wine crates, you name it! And remember: raised beds can be big or small. Even a deep container, such as a bucket or a rectangular recycling bin that was originally meant for newspapers, can yield a few veggies that grow below the soil, such as radishes, carrots, and beets, or house sun- lovers that need space for their roots, such as peppers or tomatoes. Your harvest may not produce enough to give away to neighbors, but it just might be enough to feed your family a few fresh homegrown meals.

If you have the space, but woodworking isn't one of your strengths, you can still have a standard wooden raised bed—no carpentry work required. Specially made steel or powder-coated aluminum corners allow for a relatively easy raised bed setup—all you need to do is drop in the wood, level it all out, and fasten everything together. For this task, a simple screwdriver may suffice. Or you may have to borrow a power drill from a neighbor if it's not in your arsenal of tools.

A few clever green thumbs have started companies that sell kits, meaning everything is cut to size, boxed up with all the hardware—and a set of directions—and delivered to your door. Some businesses will even build the raised beds for you.

But part of the fun is that sense of accomplishment when you've built something yourself—even if there was a minimum of handiwork required. The opportunities really are endless. Some take a little creativity but fewer tools than a woodworking project, while others can simply be set up in minutes and all you have to do is add soil—and the plants!

False-Bottom Fakery

One of Paul Zammit's tricks to avoid breaking the bank when purchasing soil to fill his stock tanks is to create false bottoms, so you only have to fill part of the container. (This can also be done to keep the overall weight of the stock tank down.) According to Zammit, the Nancy Eaton Director of Horticulture at the Toronto Botanical Garden, it's all about layering!

1: Turn over a few empty plastic pots and place at the bottom of the container.

2: Cover the plastic pots with slabs of old, rot-resistant, untreated wood.

3: Line the stock tank with landscape fabric.

4: Use binder clips or clamps to hold the landscape fabric in place while you fill the stock tank with soil.

Photos by Tara Nolan

Niki Jabbour

5: Add soil, remove the binder clips, and tuck any visible pieces of the landscape fabric under the soil so you can't see it. *Paul Zammit*

The tomatoes in this stock tank are clearly thriving in their raised bed home. *Conquest Steel*

Tara Nolan

Make a Raised Bed Using Corners

Photography by *Donna Griffith*
Corners provided by Gardener's
Supply Company

Want to learn about a fabulous invention that will allow you to have a raised bed in your yard with minimum effort? Raised bed corners. All you need to do is pick up a few lengths of wood from your local lumberyard or home center (or have it delivered). Not too much else is required for this project.

Corners allow you to have a wooden raised bed without the construction work. There are several different types of corners you can purchase from a variety of retailers. Some have a more utilitarian look while others are modern and stylish—perfect if you're putting them in a front or side yard where they will be seen.

Using corners to make a raised bed gives you a few customization options because you control the

lengths of wood that are used. So if you have a long, narrow yard with a thin strip of sun, for example, you could create a long, narrow raised bed. Midpoint pieces keep long projects stable. There are also a variety of different heights, giving you a choice of timber size.

You can even find interesting connectors, which allow you to get creative with the shape of your raised bed. In other words, think outside the box and make a triangle or a star!

The corners shown here are from Gardener's Supply Company, an online retailer that offers several corner options. These are made from a powder-coated aluminum. We used them to make a 3 × 6 bed.

2. Attach the corners to the wood.

Once you're happy with where everything is placed, use a drill or impact driver to secure the wood to each corner with the screws provided. Add the end caps to the tops of the corners.

3. Prepare the bed for planting.

Check the bed for level and amend the area accordingly.

1. Put the corners into position.

Prepare the area where you want your raised bed to live and remove any grass, if necessary.

Place the corners roughly where you want them to go and insert the boards into the slots.

Tools

- Power drill or impact driver with a Phillips drill bit
- Level
- Tape measure
- Eye and ear protection
- Work gloves

Materials

- (2 sets) 10" corners
- (3) 2" × 10" × 6' cedar boards

Cut list

PART	DIMENSION	PCS
Short side	2" × 10" × 3'	2
Long side	2" × 10" × 6'	2

Turn a Stock Tank Into a Garden

Designed by Jon Carolftis
Photography by Proven Winners

Stock tanks were invented to provide water for thirsty livestock, but these days, creative green thumbs are reimagining them as gardens for edibles, ornamentals—even for bog plants. They're the perfect ready-to-go raised bed. It's pretty easy to convert a stock tank into a garden. Even if you don't consider yourself particularly handy, all you need to do is add a few holes to the bottom for drainage—and take out the plug if one exists (simply cover the hole with landscape fabric to keep the soil inside).

If you like the galvanized metal look, you can leave it. But a stock tank can also be painted.

Add holes to your stock tank with a high-speed steel (HSS) drill bit, which is meant for cutting metal. Adding a bit of oil to the bit while you drill will keep it cool and speed up the cutting.

At the Toronto Botanical Garden, bottomless stock tanks made by a local steel company have been used to grow everything from tomatoes, peppers, and okra to leafy greens. These raised beds show urban green thumbs who visit the public garden that they don't need a ton of space to grow a successful veggie crop. "It is so important for gardeners of all ages to realize that they are able to grow fresh, organic veggies even in the absence of a traditional in-ground garden," says Paul Zammit, the Nancy Eaton director of horticulture at the Toronto Botanical Garden. "Raised beds are the solution. The harvest tastes great and the experience is incredible." *Tara Nolan*

Why Garden in Fabric Pots?

Fabric pots have been available for a while in the commercial gardening industry, but they're fairly new to the consumer market. They're lightweight and usually made out of geotextiles; that is, fabric that's porous, allowing the soil to conserve water and drain easily. This same permeability also aerates the soil and roots, which is beneficial to the plants—it prevents them from becoming rootbound, instead allowing the plants to grow strong, healthy roots. This is a bonus on rooftops or pavement, which can become very hot in the sunshine. Certain containers can end up cooking your delicate plant roots and microorganisms if they're overheated.

Fabric pots come in many different shapes and sizes. Some are around the size of the raised beds for yards that are outlined in this book. Others are more compact and perfect for smaller spaces, like balconies or a wee corner where you want to grow some produce. Fabric pots are especially useful for rooftop gardens where weight can be an issue. Some designs have handles, allowing them to be easily moved around.

TOP LEFT: Fabric pots can pack in a multitude of plants, just like their plastic or wooden cousins. *Niki Jabbour*

TOP RIGHT: Even trellises can be added to fabric raised beds to support vining crops like beans. *Tara Nolan*

BOTTOM LEFT: This willow arch, a tangle of whip-thin saplings that are rooted in four fabric pots and woven to create a leafy dome, is the perfect shady place to read a book on a hot summer afternoon. *Tara Nolan*

BOTTOM RIGHT: This herb planter can be placed almost anywhere, so a home cook can have herbs close at hand. *Tara Nolan*

Another bonus of using a fabric pot? It's great for containing voracious spreaders that you wouldn't normally want to plant right in your garden—like mint or chamomile. In fact, these pots should be mandatory for growing plants that spread. *Sean James*

Some fabric pots, depending on what's planted in them, could easily be moved into a shed or garage to overwinter and then pulled back out in the spring. Just be sure to replenish the soil with compost or organic potting soil to add in some nutrients. Others can be emptied of their soil and plants, folded up, and stored pretty much anywhere—just be sure they're completely dry before you put them away.

You can plant everything from tomatoes to root vegetables in fabric pots, depending on their size.

Burlap-Wrapped Plastic Pails

Designed by Tara Nolan
Photography by *Donna Griffith*

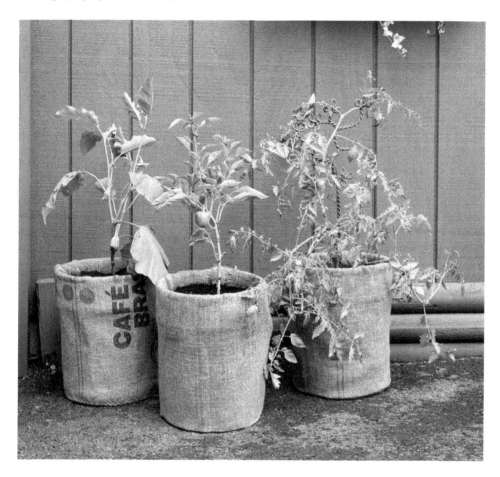

It's not uncommon to see those white plastic utility pails one might use to mix paint lining a driveway or alleyway, bursting with tomatoes and other veggies. Often, the green thumb who planted them is taking advantage of the optimal growing conditions offered by that particular spot. Even though a tall bucket full of plants would technically fall under container gardening, it's also a type of raised bed—albeit one that is more compact. These raised beds are also relatively easy to move from one sunny spot to another—or to somewhere to hibernate for the winter. (A wheelbarrow or garden cart is advised if you're lugging them somewhere full of soil.)

This project is very accessible to any level of DIY skill because it merely involves using sturdy burlap to tidy up those pails that might be sporting logos, or have signs of wear and tear. The burlap for this project came in the form of coffee bean bags, which were the perfect size to double up and wrap around the buckets. You can also purchase burlap at some garden centers and at fabric stores, and some offer burlap in decorative prints.

Tools

- Drill with a ⅜" drill bit
- Scissors
- Eye and ear protection

Materials

- Burlap (coffee bean bags or purchased in rolls)
- Needle and thread
- Large safety pins (optional)
- Colorful twine (optional)

1. Prepare the bucket for the burlap.

Drill a few holes into the bottom of your bucket. Add a thin layer of gravel for drainage, or simply fill the bucket with good-quality potting soil that's meant for edibles.

2. Wrap the bucket.

The burlap used for the pails shown here was already sewn into a bag that held coffee beans, meaning it was of double thickness and there was a folded seam at the bottom. Wrap the burlap around the outside of the bucket, using pins to hold it in place. The burlap should come right to the ground at the bottom of the bucket, and there should be some excess material to fold over the top to the inside, where it will be covered when you add the potting soil.

3. Secure with a stitch or safety pins.

Use a simple whipstitch to sew the burlap around the bucket. Or secure the burlap in place with safety pins (keep in mind they may rust when left outside over the summer). Alternatively, you can tie some fancy rope or twine around the bucket to add a finishing touch.

More Easy Raised Bed Ideas

Repurposing old objects as raised beds

Use your imagination to turn something that's lying around the house or hiding out in a garage or behind a shed into a ready-made raised bed garden. Everything from wine crates and whiskey barrels to washbasins and bathtubs can be fashioned into a garden. Just be mindful of the materials from which they're made because you don't want any harmful substances leaching into your healthy soil.

Make a barrel bed Many old barrels that were once used to hold whiskey or a fine wine are sold by the half. Talk about a ready-to-go raised bed! All you need to do is add some holes to the bottom for drainage.

Line a bed with natural materials— no assembly required! If you're completely construction-challenged, you can use logs and tree stumps to create a natural, raised border around a bed. This one was plunked right on top of a sandy area. Good-quality soil was added in the center, which enabled flowers, trees, and edibles to be planted and thrive, despite the poor conditions surrounding them.

Recycle a recycling bin Why do recycling bins make perfect raised beds? Well, they're a great height for a variety of different edibles, from root crops that grow under the soil to climbers like beans and bushier plants like tomatoes. Some already have drainage holes, and if they don't, it's easy to quickly add some. Over the winter, the bins can be emptied and cleaned, and then stacked (make sure they're dry) and stored.

ABOVE: Want to make a raised bed on a budget? Use tree trunks as your raised bed sides.

BELOW: This barrel holds an assortment of herbs that are regularly snipped throughout the season. Some, like the chives, are perennial and come back each spring. Other herbs, like the parsley, are replanted every year. The parsley also attracts swallowtail butterfly caterpillars, who munch on its tasty foliage before they create their chrysalis. *Donna Griffith*

TOP: It's unlikely you'll find potato plants at a nursery. Instead, you need to be on the lookout for what are referred to as "seed potatoes." These are generally available in late spring in paper bags. *Paul Zammit*

MIDDLE: For small containers, look for smaller potato varieties, such as French fingerling or banana. Bigger spuds can go into your large raised beds. *Paul Zammit*

BOTTOM: Make sure each piece of potato has an eye—this is where the plants will start to grow. *Paul Zammit*

Plant potatoes in a recycling bin

Many don't think of potatoes when they're choosing what to plant in their edible garden. But potatoes are quite easy to grow, and you don't need an actual garden in which to plant them. Deep containers can be used as mini raised beds for a bountiful crop of fries-to-be.

To plant, place a few inches of soil mixed with compost in the bottom of the container. Place the potatoes evenly on the soil so they're not touching. Cover with about 6 inches of soil mixed with more compost, and lightly water. Once the plants start to grow, wait until they reach about 6 to 8 inches and then cover up to three-quarters of the stem and surrounding foliage with soil. Keep doing this throughout the season until the plants stop growing.

Make a wire frame to grow

potatoes Another way to grow potatoes is to create a wire-framed, cylindrical raised bed out of fencing or chicken wire. Use zip ties or some type of clip to hold the seam closed. Line the sides with newspaper, add a few inches of soil, and plant your seed potatoes. Then cover with about 3 inches of soil. When the plants reach about 9 inches tall, add a bit more newspaper around the edges, and mound the soil around two-thirds of the plant. Keep repeating this step until you've reached the top of your raised bed.

Chapter 6

Support Your Plants

Once your raised beds are happily situated in the garden—or in your front yard, on the balcony, back deck, or rooftop—the next step is choosing what delicious edibles you're going to plant.

Despite spacing out your plants correctly, once they take off, they may start to encroach on their neighbors. Some plants, like zucchinis, cucumbers, pumpkins, and melons, grow outward on vines, wrapping their tendrils around anything they encounter. Other plants, such as tomatoes and peppers, start to grow tall but can send branches out in other directions. And then you have climbers, such as peas, cucumbers, and beans that like to work their way up toward the sky.

All of these plants can use a little help and would be happy with a trellis that they can climb. The heat-seekers such as tomatoes will benefit from some staking or caging well before they start to grow too big and lean over from the weight of their fruit. Those eager climbers will be happy winding their way around an obelisk, ladder, or other such garden support. And if you help your plants grow up, you'll save space in the garden and maintain some order between the rows.

In this chapter, you'll find a collection of stakes, trellises, cages, and other helpful supports. There are suggestions that can be used in raised beds located in a yard as well as those confined to a small space.

A Classic Garden Obelisk

The obelisk shape—four long sides with a tapered, triangular top—appears in historical monuments dating back to ancient Egypt and Greece, and all the way throughout history to modern times.

In the garden, however, an obelisk sits proudly among the plants, providing support to a variety of crops year after year. A common design is four sturdy legs set into the soil that meet at the top to form a triangular shape. Often by the end of the season, the tapered top, perhaps capped with a fancy finial, is barely visible through the foliage of whatever plant it happens to be supporting. But until that stage, obelisks are lovely, not to mention invaluable, additions to the garden.

Because of their stately stature, obelisks have long been used as decorative elements in formal gardens. However, they're especially useful in gardens full of edibles where they can help maximize space and train trailing vines of certain plants to grow upward rather than outward. And, of course, obelisks can add a great deal of visual interest and sophistication to a simple, standard raised bed.

Obelisks can be made from a variety of materials, including wood, sticks, or wrought iron. They can be simple or ornate, welded, woven, or nailed together. The obelisk shown here requires a bit of woodworking expertise, but you only need three tools to build it: a saw, a drill, and a carpenter's square. And as for materials, use a rot-resistant wood of your choosing.

Materials

- (4) 2 × 2" × 8' boards
- (3) 1 × 2" × 8' boards
- Pine screen retainer molding
- (2) 10' molds
- (1) round finial
- (1 lb. each) 2" and 2½" deck screws
- (8) 4d galvanized finish nails

Tools

- Drill
- Drill bits including a countersink bit
- Saw (hand, jigsaw, or circular)
- Carpenter's square
- Clamps
- Eye and ear protection
- Work gloves

Cut list

PART	DIMENSION	PCS
Leg	1½ × 1½ × 61"	4
Lower crosspiece	¾ × 1½ × 22" *	4
Upper crosspiece	¾ × 1½ × 16" *	4

* Cut to size

How to Make a Classic Garden Obelisk

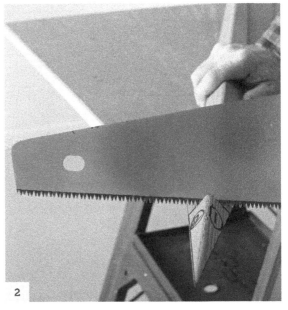

1. Measure the top of each leg.

Mark the tops of the four legs for trimming. Each leg top should be trimmed so that it has two beveled faces that meet in a point; then trim them to length. Using a carpenter's square, mark a wedge shape on two adjoining faces at the top. The wedge should be 1 inch wide at a point 5 inches down from the top of the leg. Then, using a straightedge, extend all four lines all the way to the edge of the workpiece. This will create two wedge shapes between 6 and 7 inches long. These wedges will be trimmed off in the next step.

2. Trim and finish the tops.

Using a handsaw, cut off one of the wedges to create a wedge-shaped waste piece. Then flip your workpiece a quarter turn, and cut off the other wedge. This piece won't be a complete wedge like the other one since some of the wood has already been cut away. To finish trimming the leg tops, make a crosscut that follows the two 1-inch cutting lines that you drew. This will leave a top that is 1 × 1-inch and is angled, so it will be level when the legs are equally spread out in the garden.

Make the other tops the same way. When you're finished, the four legs should fit together to form a flat 2 × 2-inch top with the leg bottoms 24 inches apart.

continued

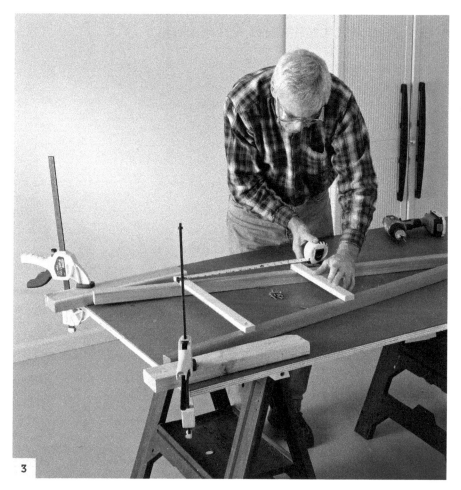

3

3. Make the leg frames.

Space an obelisk leg pair 24 inches apart from outside to outside at the bottom, and clamp or wedge them between two pieces of wood spaced to 24 inches apart. Clamp the beveled top ends together—the legs should naturally be close to 24 inches. Cut a 1 × 2 to 22 inches long, lay it across the legs 12 inches from the bottom, and then mark and cut the 1 × 2 flush with the legs. Fasten with 2-inch screws driven through pilot holes. Cut and fasten another crosspiece 16 inches above the lower crosspiece (center to center). Join the tops of the 2 × 2 legs with a 2½-inch screw. Drill pilot holes to avoid splitting the ends. Remove the assembled leg pair so that you can repeat this step for the other two obelisk legs.

4. Assemble the obelisk.

Stand the two assembled leg pairs upright with the tops joined together. Use a clamp to hold them together, and space the legs 24 inches apart. Mark two more sets of crosspieces, this time cutting them flush with the 1 × 2s. Fasten them to the 2 × 2s that are already installed, using screws driven through predrilled pilot holes. Screw the four tops together.

You can also add diagonal crosspieces on the sides to form an × pattern. Use screen retainer molding. Hold pieces of the molding in position, and mark cutting lines directly on the molding. Cut it to fit using a handsaw. Attach it in an × pattern with 4d galvanized finish nails.

Add the finial to the top. If you're using a standard finial from a home center, drill a hole for the integral lag screw in the center of the top, and thread it in. If your finial doesn't come with an integral lag screw, nail and glue the finial to the tops of the posts. Apply paint or stain to add polish to your project.

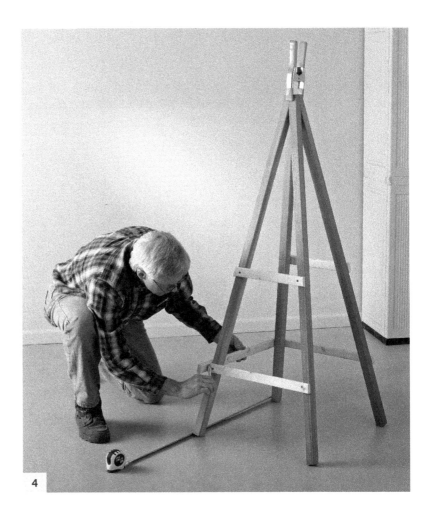

4

NOTE:

If you want the 1 × 2s to match perfectly at the corners, make compound miter cuts on the ends. Trace the leg on a horizontal 1 × 2, then draw a 45-degree line from both the top and bottom of the line, connect them on the face of the 1 × 2, and cut that angle.

A Simple Lashing Technique

If you have some sturdy sticks or pieces of bamboo out of which you'd like to make a quick and easy DIY trellis, use this lashing technique to hold it all together and make a strong, durable support system for your plants. All you need is a roll of garden twine. Waxed twine is a bit stickier than the regular version, so it may help things stay in place better.

1. Crisscross two pieces of bamboo where you'd like to join them together. Fold a 4-foot-long piece of twine in half, and wrap it around the bottom piece.

2. Pull both ends of the twine across the top cane, and cross them underneath the bottom cane.

3. Pull the twine ends back up, and cross them over the top cane.

4. Cross the twine underneath the joint, forming an X.

5. Lift the ends up, and make an X across the top of the joint.

6. Wrap the bottom cane from below and then across the top, next to the joint.

7. Wrap the bottom cane on the other side of the joint.

8. Tie a square knot and then trim off the twine ends.

Sandwich Board Trellis

There's no getting around it. Certain plants are born climbers, and they aren't going to do as well when they're allowed to simply spread out along the ground in the garden. No matter what you use as a trellis, providing an environment for certain vining veggies to climb rather than spread not only lifts the fruit off the ground, it also maximizes your raised bed space. Now you have more room available in the garden to plant other edibles.

Plants like peas and cucamelons benefit from having a trellis on which they can grow up. If your structure is sturdy enough, you can also train heavier vining edibles, like melon, zucchini, and cucumbers to grow upward.

This project takes the design of a typical sidewalk sandwich board and turns it into a trusty trellis. Two identical frames are created and fastened together using hinges. It's easy to customize the dimensions of the frames to fit the raised bed where you'll be placing the finished trellis (stronger boards may also be used to support heavier plants). For this version, pointed feet have been added to keep the trellis itself up as well as off the ground, to prevent it from rotting. Furthermore, using heavy jute or hemp twine means you can compost everything at the end of the season instead of painstakingly unwinding the vines from the rope. Then, you can simply replace the trellis with fresh twine for the next crop.

If that empty space underneath the A-frame is bothering you after planting, you can put lettuces or spinach there; they'll benefit from a bit of the shade provided by the plants climbing the other side of the sandwich board. That way, you take advantage of every bit of raised bed real estate.

Tools

- Tape measure
- Circular saw
- Drill and drill bits
- Carpenter's square
- Scissors
- Marker
- Clamps
- Eye and ear protection
- Work gloves

Materials

- (6) 1 × 4" × 8' cedar
- (32) 1¼" deck screws
- (12) 2" deck screws
- (2) 3" galvanized or stainless-steel outdoor butt hinges with screws
- 250' heavy jute or hemp twine

Cut list

PART	DIMENSION	PCS
Frame stiles	¾ × 3½ × 72"	4
Frame rails	¾ × 3½ × 48"	4
Feet	¾ × 3½ × 12"	4

continued

How to Make a Sandwich Board Trellis

1. Cut the frame parts.

Use a circular saw or power miter saw to cut your cedar to length. For this version, you will need four side pieces cut to 72 inches, and four top and bottom pieces cut to 48 inches.

2. Test-fit the frame pieces.

On a work table, line up two frame stiles and two frame rails so that the end pieces are on top of the side pieces and everything is flush. Check the corners with a carpenter's square and clamp in place.

3. Assemble the frame.

With the parts all lined up, drill pilot holes through the side and end pieces. Fasten them together with four 1¼-inch deck screws. Repeat for all sides and assemble the other frame in the same way.

4. Cut the feet.

Using scraps of wood, cut four pieces to 12 inches each. To create the pointed ends, at one end of each foot piece, use a pencil to mark the center of the board's width (about 1¾ inches from the side edges). Then mark each side edge at 2 inches from the same end of the foot. Draw a line between the side marks and the center mark. Clamp your workpiece to the table securely, and cut along the lines using a circular saw (or a handsaw or jigsaw).

5. Install the feet.

Place the top of the foot on the top edge of the bottom piece of the frame. Drill pilot holes; then use two or three 2-inch deck screws to fasten the foot in place. Be sure to make note where the original frame screws were so that you can offset these.

6. Mark your hole locations for the twine.

Using a pencil and a tape measure, mark where the holes will go along the sides, top, and bottom edges of each frame. Mark 1 inch from the inside edge. Holes should be about 6½ inches apart in the exact same place on both frames. Make sure you drill holes that are slightly bigger than the thickness of your twine.

7. Attach the hinges.

With the tops of your two frames facing each other, place the butt hinges about 5 inches from the side of the top pieces so that each side of the hinge is touching one of the frames. Drill pilot holes, and then attach the hinges with the screws that came with them.

8. Thread the twine horizontally.

Cut 22 pieces of twine, each about 60 inches long. Starting with the horizontal rows, feed the twine through the holes and knot it on the inside-facing part of the frame. Pull it across and knot it securely.

continued

9. Add the vertical twine pieces.

Cut 14 pieces of twine, about 96 inches long. Guide your twine through the holes along the top of the frame, knotting each piece on the inside as you did for the sides. As you guide the vertical length of twine to each horizontal row, keep it taut and wrap it once around the horizontal piece; then move to the next. Try to keep an orderly grid as you go. Secure it through the corresponding hole at the bottom of the frame and tie it off on the inside. You can move the twine back and forth to neaten it out after you're finished securing all the pieces. Repeat this step for the other frame.

Instead of twine, you can also use . . .

Use chicken wire (also called poultry netting) or any wire with similar hole sizes in place of the twine. With work gloves on, use wire cutters to cut two pieces that are 46 × 70 inches. Then center one over each frame and, keeping it taut, use galvanized staples to secure it in place.

For edibles such as melons, squash, and other vining plants that produce heavy fruit, use vinyl-coated fencing as your web. Using the steps from the trellis project, take about 2 inches off the top, bottom, and side pieces so that you have a smaller frame. Cut a piece of fencing to fit, and secure it in place with galvanized staples, keeping it taut as you work.

Resources and Contributors

Raised Bed Kits, Materials, Plans, and Builders

Bonnie Plants designed the Tiered Planter on page 66 and the Raised Bed with Benches on page 50
www.bonnieplants.com

Conquest Steel donated the corrugated steel sheets for the Galvanized Planter on page 76
www.conqueststeel.com

Creative Living and Growing With Bren
https://brenhaas.com

Envirolok Vegetated Environmental Solutions
www.envirolok.com

Gardener's Supply Company donated the corners for the Raised Bed with Corners project on page 120
www.gardeners.com

Lee Valley Tools
www.leevalley.com

Ohio State University Extension
https://extension.osu.edu

Portland Edible Gardens
www.portlandediblegardens.com

Rutgers Cooperative Extension
www.njaes.rutgers.edu

Seattle Urban Farm Company
www.seattleurbanfarmco.com

Smart Pot
In Canada: www.urbainculteurs.org
In the United States: www.smartpot.com

Backyard Urban Farm Company
www.bufco.ca

Urban Reclaimed Custom Furniture From Scott McKinnon
www.urban-reclaimed.com

University of Maryland Extension
www.extension.umd.edu

WallyGrow
www.wallygrow.com/

Plants and Seeds

Anything Grows Seed Company
www.anythinggrows.com

Baker Creek Heirloom Seeds
www.rareseeds.com

The Cottage Gardener
www.cottagegardener.com

Loblaws (donated gift cards to purchase many of the plants and soil for the raised beds)
www.loblaws.ca

Matchbox Garden & Seed Co.
www.matchboxgarden.ca

Proven Winners
www.provenwinners.com

Renee's Garden Seeds
www.reneesgarden.com

Urban Harvest
www.uharvest.ca

William Dam Seeds
www.damseeds.ca

Irrigation Systems

Les Urbainculteurs
www.urbainculteurs.org

Urban Irrigation Solutions
www.urbanirrigation.ca

Soil Information

The Compost Council of Canada
www.compost.org

Food and Agriculture Organization of the United Nations
www.fao.org

United Nations General Assembly document on World Soil Day and International Year of Soils
https://digitallibrary.un.org/record/765786?ln=en

US Composting Council
www.compostingcouncil.org

Gardening Blogs and Websites

The Internet provides an endless source of ideas and inspiration. Here are some must-reads:

The Art of Doing Stuff
www.theartofdoingstuff.com/garden

Beach Community Edible Garden
https://www.facebook.com/BeachCommunityEdibleGarden/

That Bloomin' Garden
www.thatbloomingarden.wordpress.com

The Bug Blog
www.jessicawalliser.com/bug-blog

Empress of Dirt
www.empressofdirt.net

#GardenChat on Twitter
www.Twitter.com/thegardenchat

Get Busy Gardening!
www.getbusygardening.com

Orchard People
www.orchardpeople.com

Red Dirt Ramblings
www.reddirtramblings.com

Tonic Toronto
www.tonictoronto.com

Three Dogs in a Garden
www.threedogsinagarden.blogspot.com

Meet Tara Nolan

Photo Credit: Marsha Z.

Tara Nolan is a freelance writer and editor. She loves to write about gardening (of course!) as well as her outdoorsy adventures on foot and on her mountain bike. Tara's gardening articles have appeared in the *Toronto Star*, *Canadian Living* magazine, *Reader's Digest* magazine, and other publications. She was the editor of *Canadian Gardening* magazine's website for six years, where she wrote for both the online and print publication. In 2013, Tara won the Gold award at the Canadian Online Publishing Awards for her "Seed to Supper" newsletter. The newsletter was created to inspire gardeners to grow their own food and then teach them what to do with the harvest via recipes, and cooking and preserving tips.

On the woodworking side of things, Tara was the web editor of the *Canadian Home Workshop* website, and later on, under a new owner, an associate editor and then senior editor of the print magazine for two years.

(Tara was so excited when her gardening world and woodworking world came together to make this book!)

In 2013, Tara co-founded the gardening website www.savvygardening.com with three fellow members of the Garden Writers Association: Amy Andrychowicz, Niki Jabbour, and Jessica Walliser. Together, these four green thumbs from two different countries and four different growing zones work to inspire both experienced and budding gardeners with innovative ideas, tips, and advice.

Tara also volunteers at the Royal Botanical Gardens, and she does work with the Toronto Botanical Garden and the Canadian Garden Council.

Follow Tara and her adventures in gardening online:

Raised Bed Revolution
www.raisedbedrevolution.com
Facebook.com/
raisedbedrevolution

Savvy Gardening
www.savvygardening.com
www.Facebook.com/
savvygardening
Twitter: @savvygardening

Tara Nolan
Twitter: @thattaranolan
Instagram: @tara_e

Index